HONEST TO GOD?

HONEST TO GOD?

Becoming an Authentic Christian

Bill Hybels

Zondervan Books
Zondervan Publishing House
Grand Rapids, Michigan

To Bob and Leah Barry,
  For discipling their daughter to be spiritually authentic.
And to Lynne,
  Who is as responsible for this book as I am.

HONEST TO GOD?
Copyright © 1990 by Bill Hybels

Zondervan Books are published by the Zondervan Publishing House
1415 Lake Drive, S.E., Grand Rapids, Michigan 49506

Library of Congress Cataloging-in-Publication Data

Hybels, Bill
    Honest to God? / Bill Hybels.
        p. cm.
    ISBN 0-310-52180-7
    1. Christian life—1960–   I. Title.
    BV4501.2.H882 1990
    248.4–dc20   89–38906
                                                                        CIP

Portions of chapter 2, "A New Dimension in Spirituality," first appeared in *Too Busy
Not to Pray* by Bill Hybels, published by InterVarsity Press, copyright 1988.

All Scripture quotations, unless otherwise noted, are taken from the *Holy Bible: New
International Version* (North American Edition). Copyright © 1973, 1978, 1984 by the
International Bible Society. Used by permission of Zondervan Bible Publishers.

Edited by John D. Sloan

Printed in the United States of America

90 91 92 93 94 / AM / 10 9 8 7 6 5 4

This edition is printed on acid-free paper and meets the American National Standards
Institute Z39.48 standard.

CONTENTS

Introduction

American novelist William Faulkner toiled for years as an unknown, unrespected writer in the rural Mississippi town of Oxford before he gained recognition. When he won the Nobel Prize for Literature in 1950, his acclaim grew. Approached later about the literary people and authors he associated with, Faulkner shrugged his shoulders and said he didn't know any literary people. "The people I know are other farmers and horse people and hunters, and we talk about horses and dogs and guns and what to do about this hay crop or this cotton crop, not about literature."

Faulkner befriended real people. Unpretentious people. People honest about their life and living. He chose to surround himself with those who populated his stories and actually lived in his intensely human fiction, rather than those who simply talked about the South, or wrote about it.

I've often spent time with people who simply talked or wrote about Christianity. I'd much rather spend time with people who actually live it.

That's what this book is about—actually living Christianity. Being authentic Christians.

Too often we Christians settle for inauthentic Christianity. We experience only partially the changes God can produce in our lives, and go through the motions that keep our faith lukewarm at best and make our Christian lifestyle mostly a vicarious experience. We are as far from the authentic Christian experience as the would-be literary admirers were from Faulkner's South.

We have just come through a decade in which the evangelical

Christian has been extremely visible politically, socially, and culturally. But has authentic Christianity been visible?

We have cried for the nation to turn back to God. Yet our daily pace and schedules speed us past the God we claim to worship, leaving our devotional lives weak and our spiritual disciplines lax. Much of our evangelism is inspired by guilt and as stereotypical as a Bible-pounding preacher in a polyester suit. We serve the church for similar wrong reasons and wonder why we lack enthusiasm. Is this authentic Christianity?

We have over and over affirmed marriage and monogamous values. Yet the divorce rate in evangelical circles has skyrocketed. Christians have allowed their marriages to die rather than accept the challenge of developing tough, honest communication. If divorce hasn't won out, marriages that maintain a front to satisfy social convention leave many Christians as wedded singles, with the pursuit of individualistic fulfillment the highest goal. Can this pass for authentic Christianity?

We have proclaimed our devotion to restoring family life. Yet many Christians start families, then expect the church and/or daycare to raise them while they protect their two-income job structure. Is this authentic Christianity?

Christian leaders heartily challenge young people to become "godly men and women." Yet too often the male models a boy sees in his church are either emasculated, weak males who lack energy and drive or macho types who exert their manhood through aggressive, childish behavior. Female models are just as confusing. While girls hear stories of Bible women who broke out of the mold and became courageous God-pleasers, they see contemporary women who are content to be people-pleasers. Do these models reflect authentic Christianity?

We have marched with placards that decry permissive, relativistic values as our culture chases after pornography and lust. But some of our media spokespeople and national ministry leaders have failed to keep their own minds and bodies pure. Is this authentic Christianity?

We claim that a good job in a good environment is a part of the equal rights package that each American deserves. Yet many Christians see work as a curse. They make no attempt to find joy in what they do or to honor God by how they do it. This says very little to the work force about authentic Christianity.

We listen to sermons about financial stewardship and the joy of giving. But we spend more than we earn as we yield to the temptation to desire more, buy more, and reach for more in a credit card culture. Is this authentic Christianity?

We've come to acknowledge vulnerability as a sign of strength and the ability to express our true emotions as a needed quality in our stressful society. Yet Christians often wear masks to hide the raw emotions that disfigure their real faces. We also applaud the virtue of physical fitness, but let it remain just that—a virtue. Pure, undefiled, and untouched. While we destroy our minds with unexpressed emotions, we destroy our bodies with unhealthy foods and inadequate exercise. Surely this isn't authentic Christianity.

We make an impression on our society by how we live, what we say, and who we are. If we hope to affect others for Christ, we must be affected first. We must become authentic. We must do more than talk about Christianity; we must live it.

The English poet John Keats said, "Nothing ever becomes real till it is experienced. . . . Even a proverb is no proverb to you till your Life has illustrated it."

I hope this book will be your guide toward that kind of Christian living—the kind of Christian living that is authentic and honest to God. In writing I have tried to point out the dangers and roadblocks I have encountered, and I have shared with you my mistakes. But I have also written of the successes of authentic Christians who are living proverbs of God's transforming power.

This book is not just a documentary of the failures of Christians who have lived inauthentically in the past few years. More than a critique of the past, it is meant to be a help for your future, and for my future, about how to live.

1

Defining Authenticity

A personal growth conference for Christians isn't the place where you would expect to see a fight. Especially a fight between leaders.

But at just such a conference I faced the unexpected. A young Christian, I was just beginning to learn about leadership. Getting a chance to observe how mature Christians behaved was just what I needed. Or so I thought.

Midway through the meeting, a question over a delicate decision led to a debate. Debating descended to arguing and finally to an ugly division. It only took forty-five minutes for these Christians to come nearly to blows.

Before those gathered could resolve the issue, however, the signal came for the next part of the conference schedule—a worship service for all the conferees. We shuffled to an adjoining room. There the committee chairman, who had been as vitriolic as anyone in the previous meeting, grabbed the microphone. Smiling from ear to ear, he said, "Scripture tells us that the mark of a true Christian is love, so let's all join hands and sing, 'They Will Know We Are Christians by Our Love.'"

That was my initiation into the world of inauthentic Christianity.

I've learned that such inconsistency is not uncommon. People too often live one way when the spotlights are on and another behind closed doors.

The dictionary defines something as "authentic" when it "conforms to what it is represented or claimed to be." Authenticity means consistency—between words and actions, and between claimed values and actual priorities. Inauthenticity means that we claim to be one thing, then prove to be something else.

Years ago I read a story about a small community that had a gigantic oak tree in the middle of its town square. The tree was the pride of the townspeople. It had been there long before most of them were born and would undoubtedly outlive them. Then one day storm winds cracked the tree in half and revealed a trunk filled with disease. A symbol of strength on the outside, the oak had been weak and vulnerable on the inside. For years it had fooled its unknowing admirers.

That story still haunts me. It scares me.

I believe the greatest challenge facing the church during the next two decades is the disease eating away at its power and integrity—inauthentic Christianity. In the pulpits and in the pews, there are too many inconsistent Christians.

Few external problems hinder the ministry of the contemporary, Western church. We have money and buildings. We have top-notch educational institutions to prepare our leaders. We have abundant resources—books, tapes, conferences, training centers, parachurch ministries. We have relative political freedom. But inauthentic Christian living negates all these external advantages.

Inauthentic Christianity manifests itself in many ways. In this book I want to examine twelve of those manifestations. We see inconsistent Christian living in:

1. A style of Christianity based more on external methods than on internal change, an attempt at godliness that lacks the power.

2. Christian men with no idea what it means to "be like Jesus," who bounce between traditional macho models and contemporary soft male versions.

3. Christian women pulled to the breaking point by the conflicting voices of our culture: Full-time mom? Career woman? Dependent? Independent? Stifled? Assertive?

4. Relationships marked more by deception than honest dialogue.

5. Marriages where spouses tolerate rather than treasure one another, where cohabitation replaces romance.

6. Parents whose outside pursuits obscure their parental responsibilities.

7. Misguided Christians who hide heartache and grief behind smiling masks.

8. Christian leaders and workers who serve ineffectively because they're doing the wrong tasks for the wrong reasons.

9. Christians who evangelize out of guilt.

10. Workers whose jobs are drudgery rather than meaningful labor, or obsessions rather than professions.

11. Budgets that are out of control because Christians don't take stewardship seriously.

12. Christians who voice great concern for fitness and health and then eat and skip exercise as if they could care less.

A PERSONAL TESTIMONY

I want to address these issues because I know how defeating inauthentic living can be.

At one time I was going through the motions of Christianity, but not really connecting with God. I was working hard in ministry, but not sensing the Spirit's fruitfulness in my efforts. I spoke of the priority of marriage, but my relationship with Lynne was falling apart. I loved my kids, but I spent too much time at the office to convince them of that. I knew my body was the temple of the Holy Spirit, but I was carelessly destroying it.

I wanted to be godly and consistent, but I wasn't making it. Like so many people, I talked a good game. Yet beneath the impressive veneer of my life was the cheap substitute of inauthentic, artificial living.

THE KEY ELEMENT

Christianity is a supernatural walk with a living, dynamic, speaking, personal God. Why then do so many Christians live inconsistent, powerless lives?

Authentic Christianity begins with spiritual authenticity—a vital, daily relationship with Jesus Christ. But a vital relationship with Jesus Christ takes time—not leftover, throwaway time, but quality time for solitude, contemplation, and reflection. Who has that kind of time?

If we want to "make it" in our fast-paced society, we have to keep moving. Like drivers of high-performance race cars, we need to rev our engines to 10,000 RPMs and keep them revved all day long. Faster. Faster. Faster.

In the marketplace, time is money. So we go to the office earlier, stay later, take work home, make calls in the car, dictate on the plane, and use meals for profit. The key to promotion, power, and compensation is to keep moving. Keep the adrenaline pumping.

It's true at home, too. Supermom can't slow down for a minute. The house is crawling with little creatures who pull skirts, color walls, track mud on carpets, and throw food on floors. Then they cry at night. Women have to maintain 10,000 RPMs just to keep up.

The pace touches everybody. Employers and employees. Young and old. Men and women. Single parents and students. Ministers and lay leaders.

I see the pace and wonder where the still, small voice of God fits in. When do we slow down and meet with Him? When do we seek His wisdom and direction? When do we enjoy a life-changing conversation with the God of the universe? When is there time?

Not often? Seldom? Never? No wonder few believers lead consistent lives.

Many marriages are examples of relationships where there is little time for personal interaction. The husband tries to boost his self-esteem by pouring himself into work. His wife has a job, too, and most of the home responsibilities. So they pass each other in the driveway, hall, or walk-in closet. Occasionally they sit at the same table, and they may even share the same bed. But there's no fire in their relation-ship—no feelings, no flowers, no romance.

Now and then, though, a couple refuses to settle for a relationship like that. They rekindle the flame. They cut back outside activities so they can spend more time together. They schedule date nights. They take evening walks together. They turn off the television. They sit down after dinner to talk, laugh, and share dreams. They pour time and energy into their relationship, and they end up with a mutually satisfying, genuinely intimate marriage.

To build a marriage like that, we have to declare war against whatever keeps us and our spouses apart. To build authentic relationships with Jesus Christ, we have to declare war against whatever worldly entanglements keep us from daily fellowship with Him. We have to buck the agendas and values of society and slow down long enough to commune with Him.

I know some people who have done that consistently, and being with them is an adventure. The reality of their faith makes them stand out in a crowd. They demonstrate the strength and security that come from a genuine, personal relationship with God. They speak of feeling treasured and protected as only His children can. Their character is deeper, their ideas fresher, their spirits softer, their courage greater, their leadership stronger, their concerns broader, their compassions more genuine, and their convictions more concrete. They have joy in difficulties, and wisdom beyond their years.

These people are energetic and creative. The depth of their relationship with God infuses every area of their lives with vitality. And this genuine spirituality frees them to be authentic in other ways.

I know I am living authentically when I sense God's power, or come up with ideas that aren't my own, or exhibit wisdom beyond my human insights. I know it when I'm preaching and the Holy Spirit does a work I couldn't do in the flesh. I know it when I'm praying and feel an extra surge of faith. I know it when I respond to confrontation with uncharacteristic humility. I know it when my conscience won't let me slip into grayness. I know it when I get home after a busy day and really try to serve my wife. I know it when I follow God out on a limb even when I'm scared silly.

Genuine spirituality starts a person on the road to a whole lifestyle of authenticity. But it's only the first step. Join me in the journey toward the consistency, depth, and fulfillment of the authentic Christian life.

2

A New Dimension in Spirituality

I backed the car out of the driveway as I do every morning at 5:45. I switched the radio from a program on ethics to the Tokyo stock closing. While I drove through the neighboring subdivision, I mentally critiqued architectural designs. I bought coffee at the twenty-four-hour coffee shop and successfully avoided the talkative cashier. As I turned onto the church campus, I formulated a convincing defense for a ministry plan I hoped the staff would adopt. I climbed to my third-floor office, wondering about the productivity of the nighttime maintenance crew. I shuffled through the mountain of mail on my desk and wished someone else could answer it.

I spun my chair around and looked out the window at the church lake, steaming in the crispness of the morning. In that quiet moment I saw the previous quarter hour for what it had been—an hour tainted by purely human perspective. Not once during that hour had I seen the world through godly eyes. I had been more interested in international finances than in the moral demise of our nation. I had thought more about houses than the people inside them. I had considered the tasks awaiting me more important than the woman who served my coffee. I had been more intent on logically supporting my

17

plans than sincerely seeking God's. I'd thought more about staff members' productivity than their walk with the Lord or their family life. I'd viewed correspondence as a drudgery rather than a way to offer encouragement, counsel, or help.

It was 6:00 A.M. and I needed a renewed heart and mind. Like a compass out of adjustment, my thoughts and feelings were pointing in the wrong direction. They needed to be recalibrated—to be realigned with God's accurate, perfect perspective.

You see, in the space of a day my relationship with Jesus Christ can fall from the heights to the depths, from vitality to superficiality, from life-changing interaction to meaningless ritual. That's a humbling admission, but it's true. In a mere twenty-four hours, I can slide from spiritual authenticity into spiritual inauthenticity.

Some years ago I got tired of this daily descent. I decided then either to do something to stop it, or to get out of the ministry. Christendom didn't need another inauthentic leader.

I began to pray for guidance and to experiment with various disciplines that would help me be more consistent. Eventually I developed a three-phased discipline that I employ every day to keep me truly "connected" to God. It's not the only path to spiritual authenticity, but for me and many of my friends, coworkers, and church members, it's proven to be a genuinely life-changing discipline.

YOU WANT ME TO DO *WHAT*?

Over the years, as I traveled and spoke at churches and conferences, I occasionally met leaders who somehow seemed to avoid the daily slide into artificial Christianity. Whenever I could, I asked what their secret was. In almost every case, they said "journaling"— the daily process of examining and evaluating their lives in written form.

Now if you think I heard that and ran right out to buy a journal, you're dead wrong. I thought the idea was ridiculous. I envisioned the saints of antiquity, with fragile parchments and ink-dipped quills, waxing eloquent in the flickering light of a candle. People who had time for that were not like me. They didn't have my schedule or live with my kind of pressure. Besides, blank sheets of paper scared me. I'm not the "deep" type; I haven't had an original thought in my life. What would I write?

Still I had to admit that too often I repeated the same mistakes again and again. Too often I went to bed with regrets about my actions. Too often I made decisions inconsistent with my professed values. In a rare moment of honesty, I faced the fact that I was living under the tyranny of an unexamined life.

At that time I was chaplain for the Chicago Bears. Occasionally before the Monday morning Bible study, I'd join them at Halas Hall while they watched films and did postgame analysis. They would go over every play of the previous day's game so they could learn from their mistakes and not repeat them in the next game.

Finally I understood. The journalers were simply telling me to do a postgame analysis! How could I expect to be conformed to the image of Christ without evaluating my mistakes and progress? How could I grow without examining my character, decision-making, ministry, marriage, and child-rearing?

Maybe journaling *was* for me.

YESTERDAY

I was still worried about facing a blank sheet of paper, but a well-known author offered a simple suggestion: Buy a spiral notebook and restrict yourself to one page a day. Every day start with the word "Yesterday." Write a brief description of people you met with, decisions you made, thoughts or feelings you had, high points, low points, frustrations, Bible-reading—anything about the previous day. Then analyze it. Did you make good decisions, or bad? Did you use your time wisely or waste it? Should you have done anything differently?

Evaluating my day would help me avoid repeating mistakes. But writing for five or ten minutes would also slow down my pace. I knew I needed that. I'm a morning person, and when I get to the office at 6:00 A.M., I'm ready to roll. The phone starts ringing, the adrenaline starts pumping, and there's no stopping me. If journaling could slow me down, I would be ready to really connect with God.

I decided to try it. My first journal entry says this: "Yesterday I said I hated the concept of journals, and I still do. But if this is what it takes to rid myself of inauthentic spirituality, I'll do it. If this is what it takes to reduce my RPMs enough to talk and walk with Christ, I'll do it. I'll journal."

And I have—nearly every day. I've never written anything profound, but in simple terms I've chronicled the activity of God in my life, relationships, marriage, children, and ministry. I've also worked through feelings, confronted fears, and weighed decisions. And I've slowed down enough to meet with God.

NOW WHAT?

The only problem with slowing down and meeting with God was that I realized I didn't have much to say. The second part of my path to spiritual authenticity, my prayer life, was amazingly weak, and had been for years.

It wasn't that I hadn't wanted to pray. I always had good intentions. I *tried* to pray. But I would get down on my knees and say, "Dear God . . ." and in five seconds my mind would be in outer space. I would start thinking of people I hadn't seen in years, making up solutions for problems that didn't exist, strategizing for new ministries, or planning family vacations.

It was so frustrating. I normally have tremendous ability to concentrate. I pride myself on being able to stick with a project till it's done. But prayer did me in every time. I would hear people speak of praying for four hours, and I would feel terrible knowing I couldn't pray for four minutes.

I would probably still be a prayerless man if a friend hadn't suggested his habit of writing out his prayers. He said God created him with a very active mind, and the only way he had been able to "capture" it and focus on God was to write out his prayers. I thought, "That's me! That's what I need to do."

Another concern I had about my prayer life was imbalance. I knew how easy it was to fall into the "Please God" syndrome. "Please God, give me . . . help me . . . comfort me . . . strengthen me . . ." I didn't want to do that. I wanted to pray with balance. So I adopted a simple pattern of talking to God that's not original with me. But it includes the four sturdy legs of balanced prayer.

Adoration

Each morning after filling my "yesterday page," I write a big A on the next page, then spend a few minutes writing a paragraph of praise to the Lord. Sometimes I paraphrase a psalm, or attempt to write a poem. Sometimes I write the words to a praise song, then sing it quietly in the privacy of my office. Often I focus on the attributes of God, sometimes listing them all, sometimes meditating on just one.

Though I've been a Christian for years, I never privately worshiped God on a consistent basis—until I started writing out my prayers. Worship is foreign to us. We were made for it. Yet because of sin, worship doesn't come naturally. We have to work at it; we have to be disciplined about it. And like any other learned activity, the first few times we try it, we feel awkward. But our sincerity, not our eloquence, is what matters to God.

There are several reasons for beginning prayer with worship. First, worship reminds us that we're addressing the Holy Majestic God and prevents us from reducing prayer to a wish list—the "Please God . . ." syndrome again.

Second, worship reestablishes the identity of God. It reminds us that God has power to intervene in any situation, that He cares about us, and that whether we're in a car, an office, or on an airplane, He is always available to us.

Adoration also purges. After five or ten minutes in adoration, I find my spirit has been softened. My heart has been purified. My agenda changes. That burning issue I just *had* to bring to God's attention suddenly seems less crucial. My sense of desperation subsides. I begin to say, and mean, "It is well with my soul. I am enjoying You, God. I am at peace."

Finally, adoration is the appropriate introduction to prayer simply because God deserves it.

Begin to worship God when you pray. Be creative. Experiment. Use choruses and psalms to get you started. Don't worry if you feel clumsy at first. God's heart is thrilled by even our most feeble attempts.

Confession

I used to be an "oops" confessor. I would say an unkind word to someone, then say, "Oops, Lord, I'll have to confess that to You later." Then I would exaggerate a story, and say, "Oops, Lord, I'll catch that one later too." All day I would add to the tally, fully intending to clear the bill later.

But later seldom came. When it did, I would make a blanket confession of "my many sins." I thought I was wonderfully honest and humble, claiming my sins like that. In reality, it was a colossal cop-out.

You see, blanket confessions are nice, virtually painless. But they do nothing to transform our hearts. It seems confession has to hurt a bit, even embarrass us, before we'll take it seriously.

One way to make confession hurt is to write out specific sins. Do you know what it's like to see your sins in print? Try writing something like this: "Yesterday I chose to wound Lynne with my words. I was cruel, insensitive, and sinful." Or, "Last night I told Todd I would play ball with him, but I didn't keep my word. I lied to my son."

It's so easy to justify our behavior: "I had a rough day. I was busy. Lynne shouldn't have expected so much from me." Or, "I intended to play ball. It just didn't work out." But we need to see our sins for what they are. Writing them out helps.

In one particular Sunday message, I emphasized the fact that we're all sinners who need a Savior. After the service, a salesman informed me that he didn't consider himself a sinner. I asked if he'd been absolutely faithful to his wife. "Well, I travel a lot, you know. . . ." Then I asked about his expense account. "Oh, everybody stretches the truth a bit. . . ." Finally, I questioned his sales techniques. Did he ever exaggerate or overstate a claim? "That's standard in the industry. . . ."

"Well," I said, "you've just told me you're an adulterer, a cheater, and a liar."

"How dare you call me those awful things?!" He was appalled by my "brash insensitivity."

As hard as it was for him to hear those words, I believe I did him a favor. I also believe I do myself a favor when I write in my journal, "I am a liar. I am greedy. I have a problem with lust. I am envious." Two things happen when we confess our sins honestly.

First, we experience the freedom of forgiveness. For years I tried to run the race of faith with chains of unconfessed sin tangled around my legs. I didn't know how much they were hindering me until I quit playing games and got honest with God.

Second, gratitude for God's forgiveness motivates us to forsake our sin. Why hurt Someone who loves us that much? Why disobey Someone who extends grace to us?

There doesn't appear to be much true confession in Christian circles. That's a shame, because exciting things happen when God's children get honest about their sin. Five days of having to call oneself a liar, a greedy person, a cheat, or whatever, is enough to drive any spiritually sensitive person to forsake that sin.

A man in my church recently began "confessing" in his journal. He said, "My sins didn't bother me much before. Now I realize I have to take them seriously, and do my best to forsake them. When it comes to this sin business, I have to fish or cut bait."

We all have to realize that sin is serious business and enlist the Holy Spirit's help in forsaking it. Then we can make progress in rooting specific sins out of our lives, and we'll know what Scripture means when it says, "the old has gone, the new has come!" (2 Cor. 5:17).

Thanksgiving

First Thessalonians 5:18 says, "Give thanks in all circumstances." For years I misunderstood this. I thought having feelings of gratitude toward God was the same as expressing thanksgiving. It isn't.

Do you remember the ten lepers described in Luke 17? They begged Jesus to heal them, but when He did, only one of them bothered to thank Him. Jesus asked, "Where are the other nine?"

I am confident that the other nine were thankful. They had to be. If you had a debilitating, terminal illness that rotted your limbs and made you a social outcast, and suddenly you were cleansed and healed, wouldn't you have tremendous feelings of gratitude toward your Healer? Of course you would. But nine lepers didn't take the time to say it. And that mattered to Jesus.

One summer I took my son Todd for a helicopter ride at a county fair. He was so excited he could hardly stand it. Later, I thought he was asleep in the car until he slid his arm around my shoulder and said, "Dad, I just want to thank you for taking me to that fair." That expression of gratitude tempted me to turn the car around and go back for round two.

When I understood the distinction between feeling gratitude and expressing thanksgiving, I decided to become a more "thanks-giving" man. I want to be like the one leper who ran back and showered Jesus with thanks. I want to be like Todd, who warmed my heart with his gratitude.

We're God's children. We have the power to offer Him joy through our thanksgiving. In my journal, I thank God for answered prayers, and for specific spiritual, relational, and material blessings. Almost everything in my life fits under one of those categories. By the time I finish my list, I'm ready to go back to adoration.

An added benefit of giving thanks is a transformed attitude. I used to be a very covetous man. I struggled hard with wanting more than I had. But a daily look at my blessings has led me from covetousness to contentment to awe at the abundance in my life.

Supplication

"Do not be anxious about anything, but in everything, by prayer and petition, with thanksgiving, present your requests to God" (Phil. 4:6). After adoring God, confessing our sins, and thanking Him for His goodness, we're in the right frame of mind to ask God for what we need.

Nothing is too big for God to handle or too small for Him to be interested in. But sometimes I still wonder if my requests are legitimate. So I'm honest with God. I say, "God, I've told You how I feel about this situation. You've asked me to make my requests known, so I have. I would love to see You do this. But if You have other plans, I don't want to get in the way. If these requests are wrong, or the timing isn't right, that's fine. We'll go Your way."

Sometimes I don't even know how to begin to pray about a certain situation. Then I say, "I don't know what to say, Lord. If You'll tell me how to pray, I'll pray that way."

God honors that kind of prayer. James 1:5 says, "'If any of you lacks wisdom, he should ask God, who gives generously to all without finding fault, and it will be given to him."

I break my prayers into four categories: ministry, people, family, and personal.

Under ministry I pray for my church.

Under people I pray for my staff and elders, and I pray for my friends, both Christian and non-Christian.

Under family I pray for Lynne, Todd, and Shauna. I pray that I would be a godly husband and father. I pray about finances, education, vacations, and other areas of family life.

Under personal I pray about my character. I pray that God will help me be a more righteous man.

Make up your own categories of prayer. Then keep a list of what you've prayed about. After a few weeks, look back over it. You'll be amazed at what God has done.

LISTENING

Journaling and writing out my prayers slow me down enough to hear God's still, small voice. The third step in my daily discipline is to listen and ask God to speak to me.

Scripture says, "Be still, and know that I am God" (Ps. 46:10). It's these quiet moments after prayer that really matter. They nourish authentic Christianity. Power flows out of stillness, strength out of solitude. Decisions that change the course of lives come out of these quiet times.

I begin with these words: "Lord, You talked to Your children all through history, and You said You're an unchangeable God. Talk to me now. I'm listening. I'm open."

Then I ask four questions. I never hear an audible voice, but often I get impressions that are so strong and real I write them down.

First I ask, "What is the next step in my relationship with You?" Sometimes I sense nothing, and interpret that to mean, "We're all right. Don't worry. If I wanted to say something I would. Just relax in My presence."

At other times He seems to say, "Just trust me. I'll help you." Often God leads me to do things I'm uncertain of, and it's easy to start operating out of fear. That's when He reminds me that He's trustworthy. He'll be strong in my weakness; He'll be adequate in my inadequacy.

Other times He tells me I need to learn more about His character. One time I sensed God telling me to loosen up. I was too concerned about trying to please Him, and had to learn to enjoy Him more.

Second, I ask, "What's the next step in the development of my character?" I always get a response from this one. There seem to be plenty of rough edges for God to chip away at! "Honesty," He'll say, or "humility," or "purity."

God has taught me that, in regard to character, little things matter. At the office, I usually do only ministry-related correspondence; the church pays the postage. Occasionally, however, the distinction between ministry and personal correspondence blurs. Once during my listening time, I sensed God telling me to be more scrupulous in distinguishing between ministry and personal mail.

That afternoon I taped quarters to two of my outgoing letters. My secretary said, "What's this?" I said, "Just pay the meter. It's important." It's such a little thing. But not to God.

Third, I ask, "What's the next step in my family life?" Again, God gets specific. "Be more encouraging to Lynne. Take time to serve her." Or, "You've been out of town a lot. Plan a special getaway with the kids." Being a godly husband and father is a tremendous challenge for me. I need God's suggestions.

Finally, I ask, "What's the next step in my ministry?" I don't know how anyone survives ministry without listening to God. Most of my ideas for illustrations, messages, and new ministry directions come out of this time of listening. I would have little creativity and insight without it.

You might ask other questions: What's the next step in my vocation? In my dating relationship? In my education?

Over time, you'll become more adept at sensing God's answers to these questions. You'll receive Scripture verses, ideas, or insights that are just what you need. Those moments of inspiration will become precious memories you carry with you all day.

The great adventure of listening to God can be scary sometimes. Often God tells me to call or write to someone, or apologize for something I've done, or give away a possession, or start a new ministry, and I think, "Why? I don't understand."

But I've learned to walk by faith, not by sight. God's leadings don't have to make sense. Some of the wisest direction I've received has been ridiculous from a human viewpoint.

So if God tells you to write someone, write. If He tells you to serve somewhere, serve. Trust Him, and take the risk.

PURSUE THE DISCIPLINES

Several years ago, I played on a park district football team. During the warm-up before our first game, I learned that I would play middle linebacker on the defensive unit. That was fine with me; my favorite professional athlete is Mike Singletary, All-Pro middle linebacker for the Chicago Bears.

The game started. When it was time for the defense to take the field, I stood in my middle-linebacker position, determined to play with the same intensity and effectiveness I'd so often seen in Mike. Scenes of nationally televised Sunday afternoon football games flashed through my mind and psyched me for a major hit.

The opposing offensive unit approached the line to run their first play. Mimicking Mike, I crouched low and stared intently at the quarterback, readying myself to explode into the middle of the action in typical Singletary style. The battle raged . . . and reality struck with a vengeance. Using a simple head fake, the quarterback sent me in the opposite direction of the play, and the offense gained fifteen yards.

So went the rest of the game. By the fourth quarter I came to a brilliant conclusion: If I wanted to play football like Mike Singletary, I would have to do more than try to mimic his on-the-field actions. I would have to get behind the scenes, and practice like he practiced. I would have to lift weights and run laps like he did. I would have to memorize plays and study films as he did. If I wanted his success *on the field*, I would have to pursue his disciplines *off the field*. Discipline is no less important on the field of Christian living.

One of the most positive trends in the contemporary church is the recent interest in the spiritual disciplines. Dallas Willard's book, *The Spirit of the Disciplines: Understanding How God Changes Lives,* has been called "the book of the decade," and I believe it is. After five years of journaling, writing out my prayers, and listening to God, I am delighted to discover additional disciplines to further enhance my pursuit of a consistent spiritual life.

Willard asserts that the key to being conformed to the image of Christ is to follow Him in the overall style of life He chose for Himself.

> If we have faith in Christ, we must believe that he knew how to live. We can, through faith and grace, become like Christ by practicing the types of activities he engaged in, by arranging our whole lives around the activities he himself practiced in order to remain constantly at home in the fellowship of his Father.[1]

If we want to be like Christ, we have to live as He lived. That doesn't mean we focus on the special moments when His character and compassion shone in the public spotlight or try to mimic Him the way I tried to mimic Mike Singletary on the football field. It means we imitate His entire life, including the behind-the-scenes disciplines that prepared Him to shine when the pressure was on. It means we "practice the activities he practiced."

What are these activities? The disciplines include "solitude and silence, prayer, simple and sacrificial living, intense study and meditation upon God's Word and God's way, and service to others."[2]

Every true Christian wants to live like Jesus lived—to love the unlovely, to serve with grace, to resist temptation, to uphold conviction, to exhibit power. But we can only live that way if we devote ourselves to the same disciplines He practiced. If Jesus pursued these disciplines to maintain spiritual authenticity, how much more must we.

In his book, Willard suggests disciplines of abstinence and engagement. The former include solitude, silence, fasting, frugality, chastity, secrecy, and sacrifice. The latter include study, worship, celebration, service, prayer, fellowship, confession, and submission.[3]

We have looked at the discipline of prayer. I conclude with discussions of the disciplines of solitude and fasting.

SOLITUDE

The discipline of solitude isn't entirely new to me. For years I've spent my first hour at the office alone, journaling, praying, and listening. After that, I spend time in quiet message preparation before meeting with other staff members. I've also made periodic use of brief getaways for solitary retreats.

Recently, however, I have incorporated even more solitude into my schedule. As I get in better touch with the natural ebb and flow of my life, I see a direct correlation between ministry effectiveness and the amount of time I spend alone. Solitude builds my emotional and spiritual reserves and increases my ability to help others.

I am a relational person. I thrive on the stimulation of being with people. I'm learning, however, that there is a danger in being with people too much. It can drain my spiritual vitality and dilute my effectiveness. I may still enjoy being with people, but I have nothing worthwhile to offer them. Lately, when I've noticed my life getting too crowded with people and activity, I've scheduled lunchtimes alone. I go to a local restaurant, eat by myself, and let God refresh me.

Because of the demands in my work, I was often tempted to schedule ministry appointments one after the other. If I had an evening meeting at church, I would return to my office immediately after dinner so I could "get some work done" before the meeting. I've learned, however, that an hour of "disengaging" may be a better use of time. If I sit for an hour in my backyard, and enjoy the evening sun, I can attend the meeting refreshed and offer something worthwhile.

What do I do in these occasional hours of quietness? I step out of the day's frantic pace, and focus my attention on God. I remind myself that He's in control. I ask for the infilling power of His Spirit. I dwell on His love. Sometimes I sit and watch my kids play, or just sit quietly with my wife. Sometimes I walk in the country. There are no set rules for making solitude count. Just be quiet. Let God do His work.

FASTING

I hesitate to write about fasting, because I'm such a novice at it. But if this book is to honestly chronicle the work of God in my life right now, I have to mention the tremendous impact that fasting has had on me.

There are numerous benefits to fasting. One is the purely physical benefit of cleansing our bodies; another is the psychological benefit of learning self-control and denial. But what has most benefited me is the increased alertness to spiritual perspectives. Prayer, Bible study, meditation on Scripture, worship—all are enhanced when I'm fasting. I think more clearly and become more sensitive to God's leadings. I feel an inner abandonment that makes me a more usable vessel.

Once Jesus' disciples complained because they were unable to cast out a certain demon. Jesus said, "But this kind does not go out except by prayer and fasting" (Matt. 17:21). I'm beginning to understand why Jesus said that. Spiritually motivated fasting seems to unlock a deeper dimension of spiritual power. Recently I've sensed God working in and through me in ways I hadn't previously experienced. I attribute the excitement and productivity in my ministry to this simple discipline of fasting.

Are you ready for a spiritual challenge that holds a storehouse of rewards? Try fasting. If you don't know how to begin, read the fifth chapter of Stormie Omartian's book, *Greater Health God's Way*.[4] She gives careful guidelines and thoroughly explains the physical, psychological, and spiritual benefits.

To people who have grown up in food-obsessed America, fasting sounds like a fate worse than death. In reality, it opens the door to freedom and strength.

A WHOLE NEW DIMENSION

I took a giant step on the path to spiritual authenticity when I started journaling, writing out my prayers, and listening to God. The disciplines of solitude and fasting have opened up new dimensions of that journey.

I can't say what it will take for you to become spiritually authentic. But I can say this: There are no shortcuts. Wishing for spirituality isn't enough. Growth that produces power and consistency requires strategy and discipline.

NOTES

1. Dallas Willard, *The Spirit of the Disciplines: Understanding How God Changes Lives* (San Francisco: Harper and Row, 1988), ix.
2. Willard, *The Spirit of the Disciplines*, ix.
3. Willard, *The Spirit of the Disciplines*, 158.
4. Stormie Omartian, *Greater Health God's Way* (Canoga Park: Sparrow Press, 1984), 125–59.

3

Understanding the Masculine Mystique

A national journalist described a new way of life that emerged for the American male in the eighties.

> Little more than a generation ago, life was far simpler for the American male. More often than not, he was family patriarch and breadwinner. His wife catered to his needs and raised his children. His word around the home was law.
>
> Not any more. As a result of the women's revolution and economic pressures, men today face a world in which macho is no longer enough. The new and improved model of male is expected to share in breadwinning and child-rearing and be both tender and tough. Where once independence and aloofness were desirable, now openness, sensitivity, and intimacy are prized. . . .
>
> Many (men) struggle to blend vestiges of traditional masculinity with what are regarded as softer, or feminine, traits. "Men are confused and searching for their identity," says Mathilda Canter, a psychologist in Phoenix. . . .[1]

We're living in changing times, and we men feel the changes. It's particularly confusing for those of us who are fathers.

> The modern father. His wife probably thinks he doesn't do enough. His boss probably thinks he takes this "kid thing" too far. His

parents think he looks a little odd cleaning the house and changing diapers. And the father himself? He may not be at all sure what kind of father he should be.

Most fathers have become reluctant warriors in a social revolution. . . . He is supposed to be the new sensitive man, caring and warm. Yet he was raised to succeed in work, not at home.[2]

A recent survey revealed that eighty percent of fathers are present in the delivery room these days, compared to only twenty-seven percent a decade ago. Anxious to excel in their new role, some men are enrolling in fathering courses that are burgeoning nationally. Current diaper ads show men holding babies, and a toothpaste ad shows men brushing little children's teeth.

When I looked over the architectural drawings for a building expansion at our church, I was shocked to see changing tables in the men's rooms. Not only had I never used a restroom changing table, I had never seen one. Times *are* changing!

These days it's not just *supermoms* who are burning out. More and more men are pulling out what's left of their hair as they strive to be *superdads*. Like mom, they're trying to do it all: career, marriage, kids, recreation.

In *Healing The Masculine Soul,* Gordon Dalbey suggests a reason for the current generation's struggle to figure out what it means to be a man. He says that too many of these young men grew up in a masculine vacuum. They grew up with fathers who were non-nurturing, uncommunicative, or absent most of the time. This left them in a literal no-man's-land of confusion about how to express authentic maleness.[3]

Out of this cloud of confusion have emerged two divergent models of masculinity: the *emasculated* male and the *macho* male.

A MISSING INGREDIENT

Emasculated males are weak, indecisive men, lacking confidence and drive.

They are more common today than ever before. Poet Robert Bly calls them "soft males."

They are lovely, valuable people—and I like them—and they're not interested in harming the earth or starting wars or working for corporations. There's something favorable toward life in their whole general mood and style of living.

> But something's wrong. Many of these men are unhappy: there's not much energy in them. They are life-preserving, but not exactly *life-giving*.[4]

They're nice men, says Bly, but they have no vitality to pour into those around them.

I am hearing this complaint from more and more women. They say, "I get so tired of being the only one in this relationship with direction and purpose" or "My husband has no energy or creativity to offer our marriage." They complain of a missing dynamic, of an essential male ingredient that seems to be lacking. They don't know what it is, but its absence frustrates them.

The emasculated male doesn't know how else to act. In her comic strip "The Sensitive Male," Lynda Barry captured this dilemma.

She depicts a conversation between a husband and wife. They are debating about who will decide their plans for that night. The woman wants the man to, since she "always" makes the decisions. The man prefers to let the woman decide, so as not to behave like a "dominant male." The debate heats up. The woman calls him a wimp and finally demands that he make all the decisions that night. The man acquiesces, but not without resistance. "What if I make decisions that oppress you? Or, what if I start being macho by *accident?* What if I *like* it? Are you sure that you can handle being confronted with my powerful masculinity, Honey? I mean, maybe you should think this over."[5]

Feminist Deborah Laake wrote, "Ten years ago we were complaining that men all feel this need to perform their macho role and think they've got to be strong and they can't cry. And now we've released them from that. We wanted to destroy sex roles, so we destroyed them, and now we're complaining."[6]

Why are they complaining? Because what they're left with are emasculated men. Soft males, feminized versions of men. Confused and frightened men who have been set adrift from an understanding of authentic masculinity.

I think the previous description of confused, frightened men fits many in this generation. Men whose fathers failed to define maleness and model its appropriate expression. Men incapable of breathing life and energy into those around them. Men who lack the mysterious male ingredient that would free them to fully engage in the challenges of marriage building, child-rearing, and career advancement.

BIGTIME BRAVADO

The macho men are every bit as confused as their softer counterparts, but they choose the opposite response. These frightened and insecure men try to convince the world that they're flesh and blood examples of raw manhood. Terrified little boys in grown-up bodies, they seek to erase all doubt about their maleness. So they dress and drive, walk and talk, curse and chew, fight and fornicate—like *real men*.

These contemporary conquistadores flaunt their achievement, power, property, muscles, and sexual prowess while doing their level best to conceal every trace of self-doubt, fear, or vulnerability. Their goal is to wipe out any vestige of suspicion regarding their identity as *real men*.

Most of us men have to admit that now and then we get caught up in this macho masquerade. I do.

Some time ago I spoke at a men's retreat out West. After my morning session, I was approached by a man I recognized as a starting quarterback in the NFL. After conversing about spiritual matters, he said, "You look like you keep yourself in pretty good shape for a minister. Are you a runner?" I admitted that I was, and he suggested that we run together after lunch.

Two hours later we met outside the lodge. After stretching out, he said, "Well, where do you want to run?" While I took stock of the trails that wound through the campground, he made the decision: "Let's do the mountain!" I looked up at the mountain towering two thousand feet above the lodge and got weak all over. He had said, "Let's *do* the mountain," like some people say, "Let's *do* lunch." I started wondering how many times he had done the mountain. Then I started wondering how long it would take that mountain to *do* me.

But did I express my concern? Did I tell him that the indoor track I run on is as flat as a tabletop? No way. I just kept stretching out and asked, "How many times?" In the end, I almost died doing that mountain. But I figured that proving my masculinity was worth dying for!

And you know what I mean. I'm not the only man who falls into that trap now and then. Some men do bold, brash, even frightening things to flaunt their masculinity. Some men use profanity and curse the name of God. Some drink beer, choke on cigarettes, and experiment with drugs.

Some men boast about their sexual conquests. I recently talked to a stranger at a gas station about sailing in the British Virgin Islands. He said, "You know, they shouldn't call those islands 'virgin' anymore." "Why's that?" I asked. He smiled confidently and said, "Because *I* just spent a week there!" He wanted me to know about more than his sailing escapades.

Some men take dangerous financial risks and get involved in investment schemes to prove their manhood. Others dominate and intimidate employees, coworkers, wives, and children to prove that they are strong and in control. Consider three major social ills of our day: abortion, pornography, and domestic violence. It is often macho-oriented men who impregnate women, produce and purchase pornography, and beat up women and children in their own homes.

Obviously this macho madness is not what God had in mind when He created man, and certainly not what He saw when He looked at His creative masterpiece and pronounced him "very good." The macho man is another distortion of true manhood. It, too, misses God's mark.

ACT LIKE MEN

What did God have in mind when He created man? What does it mean to be neither emasculated nor macho, but genuinely masculine?

The apostle Paul answers these questions: "Be on your guard; stand firm in the faith; be men of courage; be strong. Do everything in love" (1 Cor. 16:13–14).

Paul exhorts men to "be men," to act like men, and in the same text tells exactly what that means. "Be on your guard, *stand firm in the faith*, be strong!" In other words, develop and maintain a vital relationship with God. Make it the driving priority in your life. Don't apologize for it, or view it as a sign of weakness. Be strong enough to be completely devoted to God.

Paul follows that up with a second requirement for true manhood. "Do everything in love." Don't try to prove yourself by being macho. In all your relationships, learn to mix strength with sensitivity, toughness with tenderness, leadership with submission.

To a generation of men failed by their fathers and lost in a cloud of confusion, God says, "Don't spend a lifetime in aimless drifting. Don't succumb to mindless misinterpretations of masculine identity. Enter into a relationship with Me, through Jesus Christ, and allow *Me* to lead you into authentic manhood. Become my adopted sons and let me 're-father' you."

To say that God wants to re-father His sons is no empty cliché. Scripture repeatedly presents God's desire to be personally and intimately involved with His children. He wants to provide the warmth, affection, discipline, and accountability that characterize a parent's loving relationship.

But divine re-fathering is not a simple, overnight process. It's long-term, just like earthly fathering. It requires a commitment to two-way dialogue, through prayer and Bible study. It demands that sons take time to listen to the Father's guidance, and then act on it. Sometimes men will have to seek the wisdom of others who know the Father better than they do.

I know a man who, as a child, lost his father. For years he experimented with various expressions of manhood. By the time he graduated from college he had settled into heavy-duty macho, complete with pick-up truck, unkempt beard, heavy drinking, and an "I don't need anybody" attitude. A friend invited him to our church. The knowledge that he was loved and accepted by God began to chip away at his tough-guy defenses. Eventually he became a Christian. He began to study, spend time with godly men, and look to Jesus Christ as his model of manliness. He finally became secure enough with his masculinity to drop the macho props. Today he is a loving husband, nurturing father, and valuable member of my staff.

Another man grew up with a father who was too busy to spend time with him. The son became timid and unsure of himself, fearful of failure. When he became a Christian, he was amazed to learn that God had an important purpose for his life. The cutting edge of his spiritual growth was his need to stretch his abilities and use his potential. As he became more secure in God's love and sure of His power, he developed greater confidence in his God-given abilities. Even when he failed, he sensed God's acceptance, and that gave him freedom to try again. Eventually he became a strong leader and effective teacher in our church.

Adopted sons gradually will develop a more accurate sense of who they should be. Through His word and His personal direction, the perfect heavenly Father models and teaches authentic masculinity.

CONTRITE, YET COURAGEOUS

Genuine masculinity requires that individual men be "man enough" to admit their need for a vital relationship with the true God. They must make God their number one priority.

Weak men may sense their need for God, but too often they lack the guts to do anything about it. They don't dare take the risk of placing their lives under God's control. They're afraid of the unknown, afraid to move out of their comfort zones.

Macho men, of course, open their cans of Michelob, climb into their pick-up trucks, and drive down Independence Avenue. They don't need anybody, God included. At least that's what they tell themselves. But these terrified little boys need God desperately. They can't bring themselves to admit it, so they insulate themselves with lies that eventually lead them straight to hell.

Males need to be contrite enough to admit their need for God, yet courageous enough to step out in faith. It's no small thing to admit personal sin and seek a Savior. It goes one hundred percent against the grain of contemporary thought. It requires men to take a stand and a risk. Is Christianity real? Can God be trusted? You don't really find out until you try it.

A wealthy young businessman in my community enjoyed all the amenities of success—an elegant country home, exotic vacations, robust health, good friends, community respect, and a beautiful live-in girlfriend. He was the perfect self-made man. Until he learned that he had a sin problem that only Jesus Christ could solve.

Unlike many men who have "made it on their own," this young man was contrite enough to acknowledge his need for a Savior.

He began meeting with a mature Christian man for discipleship. He began to take biblical commands seriously. He began to pray about how he could use his prosperity for God's glory. He and his girlfriend established separate residences and committed themselves to celibacy while they went through six months of premarital counseling. At his wedding he made a public statement about his new relationship with Jesus Christ and his commitment to letting God call the shots in his life.

Another man knew he needed a Savior, but feared the demands God might make if he became a serious Christian. What service might God ask of him? How might God expect him to relate to people? He hesitated for months before committing his life to Jesus Christ. When he did, he sensed God prodding him to action—to pursue reconciliation with his brother, to become more disciplined in his work, to attend a men's Bible study class. Tentatively, yet courageously, he obeyed.

What did these men find? That Christianity *is* real. That God *can* be trusted. When we submit our lives to Him, we benefit from His wisdom. When we venture into the unknown for Him, we enlist His help.

God wants to father all of us until we're dead sure of His approval, His guiding power, and His promise of heaven. Why?

Because God wants us all to experience a deeper level of security. He wants emasculated men to become secure enough to confront timidity and fear, to take risks and make commitments. He wants macho men to become secure enough to crawl out from under the false pretensions and quit trying to impress people.

And God wants men to be free. Free to demonstrate toughness when a situation or relationship demands it. Free to display grit, strength, tenacity, commitment, and decisiveness under the Holy Spirit's direction.

God also wants men to be free to demonstrate tenderness, sensitivity, understanding, meekness, and humility. Free to be vulnerable enough to foster intimacy and to shed tears.

The freedom of authentic masculinity is an amazing thing to see. It produces a "divine elasticity" in men. Finally they can lead with firmness, then submit with humility. They can challenge with a cutting edge, then encourage with enthusiasm. They can fight aggressively for just causes, then moments later weep over suffering.

These are the masterpieces God had in mind when He created man. God looks at them and says, "Very good. You are magnificent creatures—and authentically male."

DIFFERENCE MAKERS

Secure, free, authentic men leave a mark—on their colleagues, friends, wives, and especially their children.

Some time ago I was at a conference with twenty Christian leaders. Our assignment one morning was to describe the person who had made the greatest contribution to our lives. Nineteen of those twenty men credited their fathers. Man after man said, "My dad loved God and was never ashamed to say that. He was secure enough to be tough on me when I needed it, but he could also be tender when I needed comfort or encouragement." As we went around that circle we were moved and challenged by realizing what a mark a father can make on his kids.

Recently my brother and I spent a lunch hour discussing the mark our dad left on our lives. Dad wasn't a perfect man, but he was authentically masculine. He loved God deeply and knew how to be firm yet compassionate.

Dan and I reminisced about the times we had sailed with him on Lake Michigan. We remembered violent storms with fifty-mile-an-hour winds. All the other sailors would dash for the harbor, but Dad would smile from ear to ear and say, "Let's head out farther!"

We talked about the tough business decisions we had seen him make. We winced when we remembered his firm hand of discipline that blocked our rebellious streaks. We never doubted it. Dad was strong, tough, and thoroughly masculine.

Yet for twenty-five years he spent nearly every Sunday afternoon standing in front of a hundred mentally retarded women at the state mental hospital. Gently and patiently he led them in a song service. Few of them could even sing, but he didn't care. He knew it made them feel loved. Afterward he stood by the door while each of those disheveled, broken women planted kisses on his cheek. As little guys, Dan and I had the unspeakable privilege of watching our six-foot-three, two-hundred-twenty-pound, thoroughly masculine dad treat these forgotten women with a gentleness that marked us.

If you're a dad, what kind of mark are you leaving on your children, especially your sons? Do you realize that your little boys are watching you like hawks? They're trying to figure out what maleness is all about, and you're their model. I hope they see in you a deep, uncompromising love for God. I hope they see both toughness and tenderness. If they do, then you have served them well; they will be forever grateful. Your little girls, too, will benefit because they'll grow up with a clear vision of the kind of men who make godly husbands.

If you're a husband, what kind of mark are you leaving on your wife? Every married woman longs to be loved by a truly masculine man—not an emasculated man devoid of energy, spirit, and confidence, or a macho cowboy who uses cheap bravado to prop up his male insecurities, but a God-honoring man who is secure enough to be divinely elastic. This brand of man can be both strong and sensitive. Such men free women to respond with respect and love.

And finally, what kind of mark are you leaving in your businesses, government, schools, and churches? The future of our nation will be bright if it can be passed on to a generation of young men who love God deeply and have the humility and confidence to lead wisely.

When men live as they were created to live, they become

powerful tools in the hands of God. Difference makers. Men who leave a mark.

WINDOW TO THE SOUL

Opponents say there's nothing quite like looking across the line of scrimmage into Mike Singletary's eyes. It's a frightening experience to peer into raw manhood—into intensity, drive, determination, hunger.

But if, as the poets say, eyes are the window to a man's soul, there's more in Mike's soul than raw manhood.

I've seen Mike's eyes glisten with tears as he spoke of the impact his godly mother had on the ten children she raised in difficult circumstances. Sickly as a child, Mike was lovingly cared for by this woman who, he claims, "taught me to be a man."

I've seen Mike's eyes sparkle with laughter while he bounced his daughter on his knee or tossed his son in the air.

I've seen love in his eyes as he embraced his wife or told of her surprise birthday celebration or thanked her for her help and support.

I've seen Mike's eyes close as he prayed for a friend who is shipwrecking his life, or to ask God's help in being a more righteous man.

I've seen his eyes search the pages of Scripture for truth.

What is authentic masculinity? It's intensity, drive, determination, desire. It's tears, laughter, love, spirituality. It's balance and completeness.

NOTES

1. Alvin P. Sanoff, Steve L. Hawkins, Gordon Witkin, Sarah Peterson, Steve Hentley and Michael Bosc with Maureen Walsh of the Economic Unit, "The American Male," *U.S. News & World Report* (June 3, 1985), 44.
2. Evan Thomas with Pat Wingert in Washington, Patrick King in Chicago, Nonny Abbott in Houston, and Jeanne Gordon in Los Angeles, "The Reluctant Father," *Newsweek* (December 19, 1988), 64.
3. Gordon Dalbey, *Healing the Masculine Soul* (Waco, Tex.: Word Books, 1988).
4. Keith Thompson, "The Meaning of Being Male—A Conversation with Robert Bly," *L.A. Weekly* (August 5–11, 1983), 16, quoted in Dalbey, *ibid.*
5. Lynda J. Barry, "The Sensitive Male," *Esquire* (July 1984), 85, quoted in Dalbey, *ibid.*
6. Deborah Laake, "Wormboys: Is He a Wimp, or Isn't He?" *Reader* [Los Angeles] (November 4, 1983), 14, quoted in Dalbey, *ibid.*

4

Women, Liberation, and the Pursuit of God

Did you know that women didn't gain the right to vote in federal elections in the U.S. until 1920? Did you know they couldn't vote in Switzerland until 1971?

In the 1960s most states wouldn't let a woman sign for an apartment lease, obtain a credit rating, or apply for a loan unless her husband or a male relative agreed to share the responsibility. At that time, many people believed it was smart for women to act dumb; some parents wouldn't even send their daughters to college. Experts told women exercise was unhealthy for them. Women running or weight-lifting was unheard of. According to a 1965 study, fifty-one percent of men thought women were temperamentally unfit for leadership in management positions.[1]

Thank God times have changed.

Today more than one thousand women serve in state legislatures. Women mayors head up eighty cities with populations over thirty thousand. Women own more than three million businesses, three hundred percent more than in 1979. More than half of all U.S. professionals—e.g., lawyers, accountants, teachers—are women. Women earned over thirty percent of all medical degrees awarded in

41

1985.[2] And women like Margaret Thatcher, Corazon Aquino, and Benazir Bhutto lead entire nations.

Most thinking men have reevaluated their biases against women's abilities. And women themselves are beginning to see their potential in a new light. They realize they have unique contributions to make to the world. The young women of today are clear winners in this changing attitude. Doors of unprecedented opportunity have swung wide open to them, and the sky is the limit. Times have, indeed, changed.

A MIXED BAG

But are *all* the changes good?

Television has been an aggressive purveyor of woman's new image. A *Newsweek* article suggests that today's TV women send four unmistakable messages to prime-time viewers.[3]

First, it's okay to work outside the home. In 1987, seventy-five percent of TV's female characters worked outside the home (nearly twenty percent more than in real life). One such character was so emotionally attached to her job that when she was suspended for insubordination, she fell apart. "You've got to understand something about me," she told her boss. "My work is just about the most important thing in my life."[4] These prime-time women don't just enjoy their work; many of them idolize it.

Second, TV women show us it's okay to be alone. "A record proportion of TV's female population lives without husbands or children. Are they lonely and miserable? Not really." As the story lines portray it, "They've grown rather fond of their independence."[5] They're self-sufficient, making it just fine—alone.

Third, TV women show us it's okay to "mess up." With self-forgiving charity, they excuse failed marriages, moral lapses, and domestic disorganization. They have serious problems just like everyone else, but they don't worry about them. "Beneath their self-assured veneers, these women carry stretch marks on their psyches. They've been roughed up by life and are coming to terms with their limits. They are flawed survivors."[6]

Finally, they show us that it's okay to "mouth off." "Do you *eat* with that mouth?" inquires Murphy Brown's house painter. He's just trying to even the score. As with most of her prime-time sisters, Murphy uses her tongue like an Uzi, especially on any male within range. Though sexual combat is hardly new to TV, it's never been waged from the female quarter with such deadly precision."[7] Ah, the joys of liberation!

Television shows us that women have come a long way. So far, in fact, they can now lay claim to being unidimensional workaholics who live in independent isolation, muddle their lives without regret, and wage unrelented verbal assault on whoever gets in their way. In short, they have finally reached depravity parity with men! I have always believed that women who aimed for equality with men were shooting too low. Unfortunately, that's right where our TV sisters aimed—and hit the mark.

FREEDOM TO CHOOSE?

Obviously, women's gains have not all been good. Women writers have recognized this.

> Consider the '80s woman as she's portrayed in magazine articles, TV sitcoms—even comic strips. She has a career. She may have a husband and child and, if she does, they are important to her. But the noteworthy fact is that she works outside the home. Meanwhile those of us who are traditional homemakers are virtually ignored.

This writer goes on to list other unhappy results of this period of women's gains—the surveys that label homemakers as unemployed, the suggestions from well-meaning friends in "real jobs" outside the home, and the low esteem women's magazines place on homemaker roles.

The author ends her article with a plea.

> All I'm asking for is acknowledgment that people like me exist. I may "just be a housewife" but working with my family has dignity and value. Isn't it time that we understood that all women can't and shouldn't live the same way?[8]

Her last line is the key to freedom from the pressures that ravage so many women today. Women are individuals. God didn't make them all alike, and He doesn't expect them all to shape their lives the same way. He wants to give personalized guidance to each of His unique daughters.

The women's movement started with two goals—to open the marketplace to women, and to give greater dignity to homemakers. Over the years it made great strides in one, but completely forgot the other. Eventually it so exalted the marketplace that it left women with no other "acceptable" choice.

Even amateur sociologists realize it was ill-advised to expect all women to fit the June Cleaver model of ideal womanhood. But it's equally ill-advised to accuse women who choose homemaking of being inferior, incompetent, old-fashioned, or unmotivated. The pendulum has swung way too far.

THE UNCOMFORTABLE SQUEEZE

The tyranny of these shifting expectations is obvious. I believe most mature women have a sense of their God-designed uniqueness and feel an inner tug to live consistent with it. But it's almost impossible to tune out the conflicting voices of contemporary culture: Be this. Do that.

For centuries men tried to squeeze women into molds to fit their convenience. Even in recent years I've seen intelligent, capable women nearly destroy their lives by taking their cues from dominant, self-seeking men. Finally and rightly women are rising up and putting an end to it.

But too many of them are giving up one burden for another. Today women are crumbling under the weight of the expectations of other women. "All women should have careers. All women should have children. All women who have children should stay home with them all the time. All women who love their children should home-school them. All women should marry."

I could go on and on. Women are hit by these missiles of expectations every day. The constant assault takes a toll.

TRUE LIBERATION

In the midst of this cacophony of confusion, God's Word says, "Do not conform any longer to the pattern of this world, but be transformed by the renewing of your mind. Then you will be able to test and approve what God's will is—his good, pleasing and perfect will" (Rom. 12:2).

I can almost hear God saying to individual women, "Aren't you tired of being stuffed into molds? Why do you put up with it? I created you utterly unique. I gave you a one-of-a-kind body, mind, and temperament. I placed within you a combination of interests, spiritual gifts, natural abilities, and dreams that no one else shares. So how can you hope to fit into someone else's mold? How can you expect another human being—man or woman—to know how *you* should live? Don't let this culture take away your choices. Don't let it bury your uniqueness."

Like men torn between emasculation and machismo, women struggle to find an answer. How should they live? How can they truly be liberated? What is the balanced ideal? What is authentic womanhood?

God says, "Ask me. I designed you. I love you. And I have great plans that are consistent with who you are. So look to Me for your cues. Trust Me for your calling."

Aggressively rejecting the notion of a single mold for all women is the first of three steps toward true liberation. The single mold idea makes a mockery of God's creative genius. He placed in every woman a unique combination of temperament, gifts, and passions that demand a *unique* expression.

When Jesus said, "So if the Son sets you free, you will be free indeed" (John 8:36), He gave every woman the second step toward true liberation. That step is freedom from the chains of sin—liberation from self-will, dead-end dreams, and rebellion against God. This inner, spiritual liberation comes when women repent of personal sin and entrust their lives to Jesus Christ. Then, like the men in the previous chapter, they can be adopted into the family of God.

I fear that some women carry a false security regarding their salvation. They compare themselves with men, who may be more profane and overtly offensive toward God, and justify themselves on the basis of their greater apparent righteousness. The Bible teaches, however, that the ground is level at the Cross. We all, male and female, are sinners who need a Savior.

That means every woman has to make a rugged, independent, courageous commitment to follow and obey Christ. As she does that, and experiences the purity, tenderness, and strength of His love, she'll become secure enough to take an honest inventory of who He made her to be.

The third step toward true liberation for a woman is to offer herself to God and say, "What do you want me to do? You created me; You know me; You see my potential. So what's Your assignment? I'm open. I want to follow Your cues and pursue Your plan, no matter what the cost. If I make every man's head turn in disbelief, and every woman in my life angry, that's okay."

THE BIBLICAL MOLD-BREAKERS

The Bible's pages are filled with women who were free from human expectations and the control of sin; they were free to pursue an adventure with God. They didn't have to prove themselves to an imaginary panel of judges or respond to the conflicting voices of their culture. As they matured spiritually, they became free to tune in to God's guidance and discern His call. They received special assignments from God and found that He provides the courage to carry them out.

Remember Deborah? At a particularly depressing time in their history, the Israelites cried out to God for a leader strong enough to reshape their nation. In His infinite wisdom, God chose Deborah and used her to engineer a political and military turnaround that eventually led the nation into forty years of peace and prosperity.

Why did God choose Deborah? Because He knew she had the temperament, gifts, and spiritual strength to handle the job. Yes, it was a rather unconventional role for a woman; but that didn't stop God from calling Deborah, and it didn't stop her from responding. Deborah didn't worry about what men or other women would think. She took her cues from God. She broke out of the mold. And with God's divine empowerment, she altered the course of history (Judg. 4).

Later in Old Testament history, an evil man planned to exterminate a whole generation of God's people. God squelched his plan through a woman named Esther. He used her unique combination of physical beauty, cooperative personality, and courage to save the entire nation of Jews. For an action-packed story, read the book of Esther. God gave Esther a high-risk assignment that took her not just to the edge of her faith—but to the edge of her life! In fact, her inner battle between fear and faith culminated in these dramatic words: "I will go to the king, even though it is against the law. And if I perish, I perish" (Est. 4:16).

That's one of my favorite "total commitment" verses in Scripture. It was spoken by a woman so secure and strong in God, that when He called her out of the mold and gave her an unusual and dangerous task, she said, "I'll do it—no matter what!" Esther was a classy, courageous, godly woman. She took her cues from God and risked her life to carry out her assignment.

The New Testament tells of a young man named Apollos who God had equipped with extraordinary teaching gifts. But he lacked spiritual knowledge, so God educated him with a husband/wife team— Aquila and Priscilla. They functioned as a "seminary faculty team." It was unusual in that day for a woman to teach a man, but God knew what an outstanding theologian Priscilla was. She cooperated and made a difference in the early church.

There are many similar stories; I'll mention just one more. When God sent His Son to this earth, He chose a woman named Mary to birth, nurture, and raise Him. God didn't randomly select Mary. He *chose* her because her special combination of temperament, gifts, interests, and passions equipped her to be an extraordinary mother. Mary responded to God's special call and provided Jesus with a safe and loving home. God's assignment to Mary was consistent with how He had made her, and she received it joyfully. Because she was devoted and diligent, she gave the world its Savior.

Isn't it obvious that there's no single mold all women have to fit into? There's no single calling God expects all women to pursue. Deborah was called to be a political and military leader; Esther, a beauty queen and national deliverer; Priscilla, a theological instructor; and Mary, a mother and homemaker.

Too many women were raised to be *people-pleasers:* Please the men. Please the grown-ups. Please your friends. Please everybody! True liberation is when women come to faith in Jesus Christ, develop inner security, and become God-pleasers—strong enough to break out of the mold, accept God's assignments, and make a radical difference in their world.

MODERN-DAY MOLD-BREAKERS

I was delighted to note that once again the most admired woman on earth is Mother Teresa. If ever there were a mold-breaker, it is this frail angel of Calcutta. Every day she gets her cues from God, and becomes a channel of divine love and transformation.

When I presented this message to my congregation, I thought of Mother Teresa. I looked at the women seated before me and thought of the power that infuses the lives of ordinary women who reject the voices of our culture and accept assignments from God. I wondered what surprises, what adventures God might engineer through a church full of radically committed, mold-breaking women. I imagined Him raising up modern-day Deborahs and Esthers, Priscillas and Marys—women who would say, "Here I am. I'll do whatever You ask. And if I perish, I perish."

After the service, I talked with a female junior high student. As I often do, I asked her what she wanted to do when she grew up. She boldly answered, "I've got my eye on your job." Then, more seriously, "I see how you lead and help and teach people, and I'd like to do that someday."

What a thrill to talk with a young woman who knew nothing about molds. She believed God could do anything through a little girl with a big faith.

Women, please do that. Make yourselves available for God's use—in the marketplace, in the home, or in whatever circumstances God calls you to. Make a commitment right now to get your cues from God. You face cultural pressures men have never experienced. You need the Spirit's help in sorting through the options and making independent choices.

If you're not accustomed to tapping the resources of God's wisdom, reread the chapter on spiritual authenticity. Learn to discern God's voice.

Through fifteen years of marriage I have witnessed my wife's struggle to maintain a lifestyle pleasing to God and consistent with who He made her to be. Lynne is an intelligent, gifted woman with many interests and passions. She is a devoted wife and mother. She also carries the title of "pastor's wife," a title notorious for the expectations attached to it. How has she dodged the missiles, blocked out the voices, and shaped an adventure that's right for her? By retreating to her upstairs office, pulling out her journal, and thinking through the options in the presence of God.

She asks questions like this: "Is this something You want me to do? Does it fit this 'season' of my life? How will it impact my family, my schedule, and my sanity? Is it consistent with my gifts? Do I want to do it to serve You, or to impress other people? Is it a godly pursuit, or a self-centered one? Is my hesitation regarding this option legitimate, or is it failure to trust You? Do I need to exhibit more faith?"

It's no small challenge to reject cultural voices, break out of the mold, and pursue God's call. But it must be done. People-pleasing is a dead-end street that leads to anxiety, confusion, and bondage. But God-pleasing is the path to peace, fulfillment, and true liberation.

NOTES

1. Maura Christopher, "America's Women: Meeting the Challenges of Today," *Scholastic Update* (May 18, 1987), 6.
2. Maura Christopher, "America's Women," 6.
3. Harry F. Waters and Janet Huck, "Networking Women," *Newsweek* (March 13, 1989), 50–51.
4. Waters and Huck, "Networking Women," 50.
5. Waters and Huck, "Networking Women," 50.
6. Waters and Huck, "Networking Women," 50–51.
7. Waters and Huck, "Networking Women," 51.
8. Angela Ward, "A Feminist Mystique," *Newsweek* (September 12, 1988), 8.

5

Truth-telling: Pathway to Authentic Relationships

Forming proper philosophies of masculinity and femininity brings us one step closer to authentic Christianity. The next step goes beyond how we see ourselves to how we relate to one another.

We yearn for relationships where we can be completely honest, open, and vulnerable. Where we can share failures as well as successes, shortcomings as well as strengths. Where we can reveal doubts and fears. Where we can find empathy and confidentiality.

These intimate, authentic relationships are exactly what God has in mind for us. He created us for relationships, and wants us to experience them at their best.

Over the years certain people have informed me that they don't need such relationships. But they've been unconvincing. Their over-done bravado has always struck me as a poor cover-up for their disappointments in building good relationships.

All of us long for deep, authentic relationships marked by integrity and open communication. But how often do we experience them? Occasionally? Once in a lifetime? Never?

During the last decade and a half, I've heard many tales of relationships marred by hidden hostilities and unspoken hurts. While a number of factors contribute to this, I believe the biggest problem is that too often we violate the basic requirement of authentic relationships: honesty. Learning how to tell others the truth is the basis of genuine relationships and the goal of this chapter.

A GREAT THEORY, BUT . . .

"If I told my boss the truth, he would blow his stack."

"If I told my husband how I feel about his constant traveling, he would get defensive and withdraw even more."

"If I told my parents how frustrated I am in school, they would be too disappointed to understand."

"If I told my wife how sexually frustrated I am in our marriage, she would accuse me of having a one-track mind."

"If I told my professor the real reason I didn't finish my paper on time, she would dock my grade."

On and on we go, explaining why we can't afford to tell the truth.

Few of us debate the biblical position on truth-telling. Speak the truth in love. Don't bear false witness. Lay aside falsehood, speak truth to one another. (See Eph. 4:15; Ex. 20:16; Eph. 4:25.) We agree in theory that honesty is the best policy. It's the key to authentic relationships.

But in those awkward moments when we stand face-to-face with someone, knowing they may not readily receive the truth, truth-telling doesn't sound like such a great idea. It might be okay for someone else, but not for us.

A PERFECT EXAMPLE

One day when I was getting ready to step out of the shower at the YMCA where I work out, I noticed another man step out ahead of me. After making sure no one was watching, he grabbed *my* towel, dried himself, threw the towel on the floor, and then headed for the locker room. I couldn't believe it!

I was upset by his action, and, being the forthright, fearless, outspoken, born activist that I am . . . I said absolutely nothing. I've learned over the years to mind my manners around people bigger and stronger than I. But this guy was little and old. He was probably free-basing his vitamins! And still I said nothing—on the outside. On the inside I was raging. "Excuse me, mister. That was my towel you just profaned. And I am more than a little perturbed about it!"

The man didn't know it was my towel he had just ripped off, so when I entered the locker room, he tried to engage me in friendly conversation: the stock market, the Bears' players strike, the weekend, the weather forecast. What did I do? I joined in the conversation and graciously submerged my feelings about what he had done. We dressed and parted ways.

But you know what? The next time I see that man, the first thought that's going to cross my mind is, "Why did he swipe my towel?" That man doesn't know it, but there's a major blockage in our relationship.

PEACE-KEEPING OR TRUTH-TELLING

Why didn't I just say, "Excuse me, sir, that's my towel"? or "Sir, did you forget your towel? I'll be happy to get you one." Why didn't I engage myself in the situation honestly?

I'll tell you why. Because it's human nature to prefer peace-keeping over truth-telling. Most of us will do almost anything to avoid conflict.

Years ago I saw a television show where a camera was hidden in a restaurant. An actor entered, sat next to a man eating at the counter, and without saying a word, grabbed some French fries off the man's plate. This scenario was repeated numerous times, and nine times out of ten the victims never said a word. You knew they were doing a slow burn inside; they clenched their fists and glared at the thief in disbelief. But they never said a word.

When people submerge their true feelings in order to preserve harmony, they undermine the integrity of a relationship. They buy peace on the surface, but underneath there are hurt feelings, troubling questions, and hidden hostilities just waiting to erupt. It's a costly price to pay for a cheap peace, and it inevitably leads to inauthentic relationships.

ENTER THE TUNNEL

In his book *The Different Drum*, Scott Peck presents an interesting theory about relationships. He says God designed us to yearn for open, honest, authentic relationships—"communal" relationships. But because we choose peace-keeping over truth-telling, we end up in "pseudocommunal" relationships instead.

These are marriages, family relationships, or friendships that are strictly surface level. No one says anything "unsafe." They never discuss misunderstandings, reveal hurt feelings, air frustrations, or ask difficult questions. The underlying rule in pseudocommunity is: *Don't rock the boat. Don't disturb the peace.*

But it's a counterfeit peace. Misunderstandings arise, but they're never resolved. Feelings beg to be shared, but they're not. Offenses occur, but nobody talks about them. Doubts about the other's integrity creep in, but they're never dealt with.

In time such relationships deteriorate. The secret agendas of hurt and misunderstanding lead to detachment, distrust, and bitterness. Feelings of love begin to die. It's the story of too many marriages, family relationships, and friendships.

Peck says the only antidote to pseudocommunity is chaos—I call it "the tunnel of chaos," where hurts are unburied, hostilities revealed, and tough questions asked. Skiers know that if they want to drive from Denver to Vail, Colorado, they have to go through the Eisenhower Tunnel. It doesn't matter how much they dislike tunnels. If they want to make it to Vail, they have to go through that tunnel. Likewise no matter how unpleasant the tunnel of chaos is, there's no other route to authentic relationships.

A TALE OF TWO DOGS

Awful things can happen in that tunnel. One person in a relationship may decide to leave the counterfeit peace of pseudocommunity by revealing a long-concealed wound that hampers the relationship. Timidly he enters the tunnel. It's scary, but he cares about the relationship and wants to improve it. So he takes the risk.

What happens? All heck breaks loose! The counterfeit peace shatters in an explosion of hostility that feels terrible.

I know.

Early in our marriage I realized that Lynne and I were in pseudocommunity. I didn't know the term back then, but I knew I felt detached from Lynne because of grievances I had stored up against her. I'm a fairly confrontive person, and I decided to air these issues so I could relate to Lynne more authentically.

During a vacation at a beautiful lake in Wisconsin, I asked her to join me on the dock. It was a lovely evening; the water shimmered in the golden glow of the sinking sun. It was the perfect time for a little "heart to heart." I carefully articulated the truth as I saw it. My communication skills left a bit to be desired, but I spoke as lovingly and sensitively as I knew how to at that time. I fully expected a comfortable conversation and a heartfelt apology.

Instead I watched as my beautiful, spiritual, well-mannered, five-foot-four, one-hundred-and-five-pound French poodle turned into a Doberman pinscher. With both ears laid back, her eyes on fire, and her teeth bared, she let me have it! I couldn't believe it.

PLAN B

I decided then and there that truth-telling was a bad idea. Maybe pseudocommunity wasn't ideal, but it sure beat chaos. I wanted my French poodle back! I decided to opt for Plan B. Submerge the feelings. Suppress the truth. Ignore the issues. Back off. Keep the peace.

In all fairness to Lynne, I have to tell you that her attempts at truth-telling had met with the same resistance. More than once in the early years of our marriage, she tried to tell me how deeply my workaholism was wounding her. More than once, I stonewalled her. I suggested that she fix her insecurities, grow up, and "help me instead of hold me back." Eventually she too settled for Plan B.

What did we accomplish? We simply postponed our appointment in the tunnel. We thought that if we ignored our problems they would eventually go away. Instead they turned over and over in our minds, like meat on a rotisserie grill, and became more and more inflamed. The chaos we eventually faced made the evening on the dock look like child's play.

We made the mistake of believing that the other's initial defensiveness was the end of the world, so we backed off. In reality, the defensive reaction was simply the opening to the tunnel of chaos. If we had entered the tunnel, and then talked our problems through to a resolution, we could have moved into true community. But we were so frightened that we made a U-turn and headed back into years of pseudocommunity.

Thank God, our frustration eventually led us to tell the truth and let the chips fall. We did find out that the tunnel of chaos is a frightening place to be. But when we came out the other side, we realized that going through the tunnel was a small price to pay for the open communication and freed-up love of an authentic relationship. It was worth it.

Before I share some of the guidelines we found helpful in telling the truth, I want to introduce you to a few folks who don't want to pay the price for open communication. Oh, they're all for authentic relationships. They desperately want to enjoy true community with their family and friends. But they're convinced they can get there without going through the tunnel. They know how traumatic truth-telling can be, so they've come up with some "safer" methods.

Henry the Hintdropper

Henry believes outright truth-telling is crude and brash and upsetting. So he devises an ingenious plan to accomplish the same objective, without actually having to tell the truth.

Henry has been in pseudocommunity with his wife since she decided to reenter the marketplace. She's having a hard time juggling a full-time job, two junior high kids, a husband, a house, and meals, and Henry is having a hard time adjusting to her new schedule. He's feeling a bit neglected by his once attentive wife. At first he tries to submerge his frustration, and not say anything. But eventually detachment and bitterness set in, and he decides he has to do something. He wants to move out of pretense and back into marital intimacy where he belongs.

He could say, "Honey, I'm hurt. I feel neglected. I know you're juggling a lot, but we can't go on like this. How can I help? What solution can we come up with?"

But that's not Henry's style.

One night as his wife scrambles to get dinner on the table, Henry looks over the top of his *Wall Street Journal* and says, "You know, honey, I'm thinking of buying stock in Stouffer's frozen dinners." *Oh, that was a good one,* he thinks to himself. She says, "What did you mean by that, Henry?" He says, "Oh, nothing. I just heard some takeover rumors." He only wants to plant a seed, you know.

Later that evening Henry tells his wife that a friend at work finds romantic notes tucked in his pocket three times a week. "That's some woman Frank's married to." He thinks he's really communicating now. He's on a roll! The capper comes when he tells his wife he saw an ad for a new outfit called "Rent-a-Wife."

While Henry congratulates himself on his clever subtlety, his wife contemplates the joys of homicide. Eventually she says, "Okay, Henry, cut the games. Enough cute stuff. If you have a problem, let's talk about it!" She didn't appreciate his hint-dropping ploys, and in an instant, they're smack dab in the middle of the tunnel.

Hint-droppers want to avoid the tunnel at all costs, but they only postpone the meeting, and in the process, they add insult to injury. On top of the initial problem they heap all the damage done during the hint-dropping era.

Mary the Manipulator

Mary has a serious marriage problem—her husband. He's a mild-mannered, peace-loving, laid-back man who's not nearly as motivated or energetic as Mary thinks he should be. And she should know, shouldn't she? I mean, isn't *she* the standard by which everyone else is to be evaluated?

After six years of marriage to a man who uses only sixty-watt light bulbs, she's had it. It's time to do something—to "should" him into action. "Carl, you should do something. Every time I see you, you're vegetating." "Carl, you should spend more time with Jimmy. He's having trouble with math again." "Carl, you should take night classes and improve yourself." "Carl, you shouldn't spend so much time watching TV." "Carl, you should take up jogging." She's like a recording: Carl, you should. Carl, you shouldn't.

Mary the Manipulator hopes to reshape Carl into someone with whom she can experience true community. Little does she know what's going on in Carl's head while he lies on the couch listening to her rantings. He's marveling at her arrogance and moralizing. He's astounded by her not-so-well-concealed attempts to re-create him. And this mild-mannered man is on the brink of coming to life!

He's about to stand up and say, "Okay, Mary, enough is enough. I'm different from you, Mary—no better or no worse, just different. God made me this way, and you have no right to try to remake me in your image. If you would like me to take up jogging, then feel free to tell me that. You have a right to express your desires. But don't tell me I *should* do it. Only God can tell me what I should and should not do. Understand?"

Mary wanted to avoid the tunnel, but she's in it now! And Carl's hoppin' mad about her manipulating ways. Her "safer method" got her in deep weeds.

Gary the Guilt-tripper

Gary's trump card is one we're all familiar with. "Gee, Fred! After *all* I've done for you, you refuse to do this one little thing for me. How *could* you?" Or, "Jim, what do you mean, you can't go with me?! I was *depending* on you. Now, I'll have to go alone, and I'll probably get mugged or something!" Or, "Well, if *that's* all your mother and I mean to you . . . okay then . . . no problem from us." Or, as I heard recently, "It's your choice, Pastor Hybels. If you won't respond to my request, I'll go to a church where the pastor *loves* his people. There's no reason to stay at *this* church!"

Don't you just love to be spoken to like that? Nothing brings out the worst in us like a good old-fashioned guilt trip. The guilt-tripper's goal is to get what he wants, and often he does, but always at the expense of authenticity. People may give in to the guilt-tripper's demands, but the wheels of rebellion are set in motion, and the ultimate destination is the tunnel of chaos.

MORE NOT-SO-NOBLE CHARACTERS

Ivan the Intimidator gets real upset when his feelings get hurt. He's not content just to talk about it; he wants to "blow somebody away." He intimidates other people into submission. Ivan spends half his life in the tunnel and doesn't even know it.

When Steve the Stonewaller gets hurt, he pouts, slams doors, clumps around with his head down, and groans instead of breathes. Sooner or later people notice the commotion and express concern. "Hey Steve, do we have a problem? Is there something you want to talk about?" Steve says, "We don't have a problem. And if we do, I *don't* want to talk about it." How's that for truth-telling?

Steve's sister, Sarah, plays the same game from a slightly different position. "Is something wrong, Sarah?" "No," she whimpers. "Are you sure?" She nods an unconvincing "yes." You walk away to the sound of her woeful sighs.

GUIDELINES FOR TRUTH-TELLING

Recently my daughter and I were walking in the country and I said, "Honey, I want to know everything that's going on in that little mind of yours. If you have a problem with me about anything, I want you to tell me. If you have some hard questions to ask me, ask them." And she did. We talked about everything under the sun—things that were easy to talk about, and things that were difficult. But during that precious hour, community blossomed. Love grew. Our relationship was cemented.

Authentic relationships provide some of the greatest joys of life, but we'll never experience them if we play the games just discussed. We need to deal openly with the wedges that occasionally get stuck in even the best relationships.

Here are some practical suggestions for negotiating the tunnel so we can move into true community.

First, identify the real obstacle. Before you blurt out an unedited, "Hey, Buddy, I've got a problem with you," take time to determine the real issue. Is it hurt feelings? Is it a history of dishonesty? Do you feel neglected? Misunderstood? Identify it, then talk to the Lord about it. Sort it out. Some people find it helpful to organize their thoughts on paper.

Second, arrange to meet the person face-to-face as soon as possible. Jesus tells us that if we have a problem in a relationship we should meet with that person in private (Matt. 18:15). Paul says we should do it as soon as possible. "Do not let the sun go down while you are still angry" (Eph. 4:26). The longer we stay in pseudocommunity, the more the relationship deteriorates.

Third, when you meet, affirm the relationship before you open up the agenda. If you're meeting with your spouse, say, "Look, honey, I love you and I value our relationship. I want our marriage to be all it can be, and I believe it has the potential to be mutually satisfying in every way. But I need to talk to you about a few things that are standing in the way."

If you're meeting with an employer, say, "Sir, I value this job, and I want to have a good working relationship with you. I can't, though, until I deal with some frustrations I feel. Would you please listen to me so we can clear up some misunderstandings."

Fourth, make observations rather than accusations. Human beings tend to do what animals do when they're attacked. They strike back. Don't put up your dukes and start throwing punches. Say, "Look, I'm feeling hurt by some things you did. You probably didn't intend to hurt me, but that's what I feel. Can we talk about it?" Or "I'm sensing a change in our relationship. I don't feel as comfortable with you anymore. I'd like your input." That opens the way for dialogue that can lead to true community.

A man in my church gave me permission to quote the following letter.

Dear Bill:

My company's vice president is in the habit of riding roughshod over me, and I've developed the habit of swallowing my feelings about it. Well, today my boss did it again. This time I gave my reaction to the Lord, and the Lord produced flashbacks of some of your recent messages on truth-telling.

I decided not to submerge my anger any longer. I walked into my boss's office, trusting the Lord for the right words to say. The resulting conversation was refreshingly honest—and a breakthrough for me and my employer. How thankful I am for God's plan of telling the truth.

That man said, "Enough is enough. I've had it with pseudocommunity." He walked into the tunnel trusting God, played no games, and came out the other side on the path to a relational authenticity.

AN HONEST LOOK

Just for a moment, think of the key people in your life: spouse, children, parents, friends, neighbors, coworkers. Ask yourself two questions about your relationship with them. Are you telling the truth to these people? Or are you in pseudocommunity, where the basic value is peace-keeping at any cost?

Chances are, some or many of those relationships are pseudorelationships. They're blocked by grievances or concerns you're afraid to talk about because you know a confrontation will force you into the tunnel of chaos.

If that's true, please remember this: The counterfeit peace of inauthentic relationships always deteriorates into relational death. Therefore, you *must* pursue truth-telling; you *must* risk the tunnel. Walk into it and wrestle with the truth. Use careful, honest forms of communication, then trust God to bring you out the other side. As unpleasant as it seems, entering this tunnel is the first major step toward relational authenticity.

THE FLIP SIDE

There is, of course, a flip side to truth-telling. It's called truth-hearing.

What goes through your mind when someone to whom you've posed a question says, "Well, do you want the truth, or should I lie and make you feel good?" Doesn't a part of you want to scream, "I'll take the lie! Make me feel good!"

Part of me says that, but another part says, "No, I better not do that. I need to hear the truth."

Through my office window I can see our recently completed wedding chapel. I remember when we had the soil borings done prior to starting construction. The soil analyst said, "Do you want the truth about the soil under the chapel area, or should I lie and make you feel good?"

Although we wanted to believe that all was well under that meticulously manicured lawn, we knew that if we hoped to build on a solid foundation, we had to know the truth. As it turned out, his truthful words meant added inconvenience and expense. But as I look at that beautiful chapel and anticipate years of use, I'm glad we requested, received, and responded to the truth.

Some time ago my mother saw her doctor. In her typical, easygoing fashion she asked, "So, how am I doing?" He said, "Do you want the truth, or should I lie and make you feel good?" She passed on the "feel good" option and asked for the truth. He said she had cancer and needed major surgery immediately. So she gathered the family around her, had the surgery, and now, several years later, has a clean bill of health. We're all *very glad* she requested, received, and responded to the truth.

When you're constructing a building or making medical decisions, it pays to hear and respond to the truth—even if the short-term effect is pain, discomfort, expense, heartache, or chaos. The same is true when you're building relationships. It pays to hear and respond to the truthful words of others—even if they're hard words that upset apple carts, rock boats, and cut to the core. A relationship built on anything less than truth is destined for disaster.

We need to hear the hard words of truth. But how can we overcome our natural, human instinct to reject them?

SELF-DEFENSE

During a baseball game I saw a batter hit a fast ball straight back at the pitcher. In the split second the ball was in the air, the pitcher reflexively lifted his glove and caught the sizzling line drive. The commentator said, "The pitcher caught the ball in self-defense." He wasn't going after the ball; he simply responded to protect himself from an oncoming missile.

Most of us tend to respond reflexively to the hard-to-hear, truthful words that from time to time fly at us. Almost before they're uttered, we call out our self-protective weapons of denial, retaliation, and rationalization.

"Bill, I'd like to talk to you about something." The second I sense that harsh words might be coming, I activate my denial weapons. "He's got the wrong guy. Whatever he thinks I did, I didn't do. I couldn't possibly do anything to offend him."

Then I fire up the retaliation machine. "If he points the finger at me, he'll be in big trouble. He hasn't lived a perfect life, either, you know. If he starts dragging out my dirty laundry, I'll dump his clothes basket all over the neighborhood. He'll be sorry he tangled with me!"

Finally, my deluxe rationalizer kicks in. I don't even know what the issue is yet, but my rationalizer says, "There are two-hundred-fifty ax murderers loose on the street, and you're coming after me for some petty misdemeanor?" It's so easy for the issue to become overshadowed by our reflexive, immature need to protect ourselves from the hard truth.

Too often truth-telling sessions degenerate into shouting matches, pouting contests, and power plays. Why? Because we can't stand to say these words: "You're right. I'm sorry." We would rather have people lie and make us feel good than tell us truths that make us uncomfortable.

GUIDELINES FOR TRUTH-HEARING

James 1:19–20 says, "Everyone should be quick to listen, slow to speak and slow to become angry, for man's anger does not bring about the righteous life that God desires." An appropriate paraphrase might be: "Be quick to hear the hard words that people bring to you. Then be slow to react. Don't rush into denial, retaliation, and rationalization."

Our challenge is to convert the energy once used by our self-defense machines into listening power, vulnerability power, contemplation power. We need to say to ourselves, "Before I fire up the machines, I'm going to quiet myself and listen. I'm going be quick to hear, slow to speak, and slow to anger. I'm going to search for the truth in what this person is saying, and learn from it."

My goal is to become such a truth-lover that I willingly listen to even the hardest words. I want to deal more with issues and truth than with ego and fragile feelings. That doesn't mean I have to bow to every word of criticism that comes my way. It does mean, however, that if people bring me words that are true, I owe it to them—I owe it to me—to listen.

Let me give you a challenge. Go to someone you know well and trust—a spouse, parent, child, friend, or fellow worker—and say, "If you knew I wouldn't get defensive and angry, what hard truth would you like to tell me? Is there something you've been wanting to say to me, but haven't dared to because you were afraid of my reaction? Well, now's your chance."

Then sit back and listen. Don't say anything. Don't shake your head in disbelief. Don't pound your fist on the table. Just let the words sink in and do a work in your heart. I know from experience what a valuable exercise this can be. More than once a friend's hard words have revealed inconsistencies and sins I was unaware of. I'm a better man for every time I took such words to heart.

BUT WHAT IF . . .

I've given several sermons about truth-telling, and every time I've been asked the following question: "What do you do when you're in a relationship with someone who simply will not engage in truth-telling? What if he or she absolutely refuses to hear hard words?" This is a particularly sticky issue when it pertains to marriage.

Here's my response. First, make sure you are really speaking the truth in love. Be careful to follow the guidelines given earlier: Identify the issue, meet privately as soon as possible, affirm the relationship, and make observations rather than accusations. Truth-telling sessions are sabotaged by people who are long on truth and short on love.

Second, make sure you have received and responded to the issues the other person has communicated to you. Do a real "gut-check" on this one. Did you listen and seek the truth in the other person's concerns? Or did you get angry? Did you slip into denial, retaliation, or rationalization? You can't ask more from another person than you're willing to do yourself.

Third, realize that sometimes deception runs so deep in us that it necessitates repeated sessions on telling the truth. Years ago I had a falling out with a friend, and because neither of us were as committed to giving and receiving truth as we are now, we remained unreconciled for five years. When we finally attempted to reconcile, it required over a year of agonizing, monthly meetings. At times it seemed hopeless, but we stuck with the process, and it worked. Today we enjoy a close friendship built on love and trust.

What's the message here? *Be patient.* Trust the process. And don't be surprised if God does graduate-level character transformation in you as you devote yourself to relational healing.

EXCEPTIONAL CASES

I would like to end this chapter here, but integrity demands I add one more point. Sometimes deception runs so deep in a relationship that temporary suspension of the relationship may be necessary. This is particularly true when there is substance abuse (drugs or alcohol), emotional or physical abuse, immorality, financial deception, or spiritual hypocrisy. If long-term, consistent truth-telling fails to result in relational healing, there may be no acceptable alternative.

A young woman in my church had suffered extreme child abuse at the hands of her parents. Her counselor encouraged her to talk with her parents about it to open the way for personal healing and relational authenticity. Repeatedly her parents denied any wrongdoing, and accused her of trying to destroy their lives and reputation. Their deception so traumatized her and thwarted her healing process, that her counselor recommended a temporary suspension of all attempts to relate to them.

Occasionally our church counselors recommend that spouses of alcoholics temporarily suspend their relationship with their husband or wife. Deception is often so ingrained in alcoholics' thought processes that honest communication is absolutely impossible. Only detox-ification can free them to relate authentically. It often takes the dramatic suspension of a significant relationship to force them to get the help they need.

If you're trapped in a relationship so steeped in deception that honest communication seems impossible, seek the counsel of godly people. With their help, determine the course of action that will best serve both you and the other person. If temporary suspension of the relationship is necessary, pray that God will use it to shatter the deception and open the way for future reconciliation.

TRUTH OR CONSEQUENCES

My life is filled with people. I spend time with people at church, I meet with people when I travel, I work out with people at the YMCA, I socialize with people in the community, and I live with people in my home. It's probably the same for you.

So what does that say about relationships? That they ought to be one of our primary concerns. The shape of our relationships determine, in large degree, the shape of our lives. That's why learning to give and receive hard words is so important.

I know it's uncomfortable. I know the truth can be threatening. I know the tunnel to authenticity is frightening. But there's no other way.

It's hard words or hidden hostilities. It's revealed pain or buried resentment. It's tough questions or unspoken doubts.

It's truth . . . or the consequences.

6

Mutually Satisfying Marriage

Through a strange turn of events, Lynne and I recently found ourselves holding hands and skating around a 1950s-style roller rink in southern Wisconsin. Several times throughout the evening it struck me that I would rather be holding hands and skating with her than with any other woman in the world. Though I probably shouldn't have been, I was amazed by the strength of my attraction for her.

I first met Lynne twenty years ago. We were seventeen, and believe it or not, we were at a roller skating party. I saw her out of the corner of my eye, carefully checked her out, and was just about to ask her to skate when the announcer stopped the music and said the next skate was ladies' choice. Much to my delight, the first girl to invite me to skate was Lynne.

So began five years of courtship that led to the marriage I count as one of the greatest blessings of my life. Lynne and I enjoy an authentic love relationship that provides mutually satisfying companionship and intimacy.

But you know from reading the previous chapter that our marriage wasn't always that way. The flames that flickered twenty years ago nearly died many times, and they didn't hit their present bonfire level without a lot of fanning of the coals.

During those long years of working out our marriage, we learned a lot about the difference between an authentic and an inauthentic marriage. In an authentic marriage, you genuinely delight in one another's uniquenesses. You also know how to give and receive love in such a way that you both feel loved. And you enjoy the fun, romantic side of your marriage so much that you don't have any trouble keeping your affections centered at home.

In an inauthentic marriage, you may talk about treasuring your spouse's uniquenesses, but in reality you barely tolerate them. You may try to offer one another love in meaningful ways, but often you and your spouse end up feeling unloved and misunderstood. And fun and romance? It's something you wistfully long for, but it's never more than a dream. The grass always looks greener somewhere else.

In this chapter I want to offer three suggestions for moving from an inauthentic marriage to an authentic one. First, learn to understand and appreciate inborn temperament differences. Second, learn the "language of love." And finally, take practical steps to nurture the fun side of marriage.

A RUDE AWAKENING

I dated Lynne off and on for five years, but it was not until after the wedding that I found out the awful truth. Lynne was strange. She was not normal like me.

To begin with, she turned out to be a near-recluse. I would come home from an exciting, energizing day at work and suggest we invite friends over for the evening, and Lynne would say, "Sorry, I don't feel like it. I'd rather have a quiet evening alone."

I would say, "Who did you talk to today?" and she would say "No one."

I would say, "Why don't you plan a getaway with your friends this weekend," and she would opt out because of a good book she was "dying to read."

I did my best to transform her relational life. I did everything I could to encourage her to be more social—like me. But to no avail. She persisted in being a hermit.

She even accused me of being a "relationship junkie." She said I had too many relationships and didn't take any of them seriously enough. She stooped so low as to suggest that I treated our marriage too casually, like just another relationship in my list of many.

Then there was the issue of her oversensitivity. One night we watched a television movie about a man who died in an airplane crash on his way to propose marriage to a beautiful, young paraplegic. You would have thought Lynne's best friend had just died. She couldn't sleep. She cried all night. When I tried to talk sense into her, and reminded her it was just a movie, she accused me of hard-heartedness. "Can't you feel the pain of that tragic, broken romance?"

I would tell her about a couple I met whose finances were in shambles, and she would ask me what I was going to do about it. I'd say, "Nothing. It's their problem. They made the wrong choices. They created the debt. Now it's their responsibility to scrimp and save their way out of it."

She would say, "But they were young. They probably didn't know any better. If you got yourself in a jam like that, wouldn't you hope somebody would help you out?" She was always worrying about how people felt, always wanting to take responsibility for their problems.

To me it seemed obvious that sometimes people have to learn lessons the hard way. Sometimes forcing them to do that is just what they need. She said I just didn't care about people. That I was heartless and cruel. That I had no feelings.

Then there was the planning issue. She always had to have everything planned. The word *spontaneity* was not in her vocabulary. Whenever I said, "Let's do 'such and such'," she had to take time to "get ready" or "make arrangements." And when I changed plans or came up with a spur-of-the-moment idea, she accused me of being unpredictable and disorganized!

I don't know why I had been so blind to all this while we were dating. It was suddenly so clear that this girl had problems.

An ancient Greek legend tells of a Cyprian king named Pygmalion who found a unique way of solving potential marital differences. He became so frustrated with his inability to find the right woman to marry that he decided to sculpt one. Out of the most exquisite ivory he could find he fashioned the woman of his dreams. When he was done, he bowed and prayed. The ivory woman miraculously came to life. Pygmalion took her as his wife and they lived happily ever after.

It's easy to see why that legend endured. Wouldn't you love to custom-design a wife, or a husband? Wouldn't it be fun to take the chisel and chip away until you had the man or woman of your dreams?

That's exactly what many of us try to do to our spouses. For years I tried to chip away at what I thought were Lynne's rough edges, those flaws that made her think, or behave, or respond differently from me. I truly believed that if I could just get her to be more like me, we could have a decent marriage. She thought the same about me. We each thought that we were the standard by which all others should be judged.

But God intervened. He used a book called *Please Understand Me: Character and Temperament Types* by David Keirsey and Marilyn Bates to reveal our mutual deception.

DIFFERENT ISN'T BAD

In the 1920s Carl Jung took a new look at the old theory that just as people are born with differing physical traits—tall or short, brown-eyed or blue-eyed, right-handed or left-handed—so they are born with differing temperament traits. In the 1950s Isabel Myers and Katheryn Briggs expanded Jung's work and devised the Myers-Briggs Type Indicator test, a tool for identifying personality types based on various combinations of inborn temperament traits.

Please Understand Me is an in-depth look at Jung's theory and the applications made by Myers and Briggs. Lynne and I read it one year on vacation, and to say it revolutionized our marriage is no exaggeration. It dispelled the notion that there is one standard of "normalcy" and whoever doesn't fit it is wrong.

The theory proposes that people approach four selected areas of life in ways that are fundamentally different—but equally right. These different ways of behaving are called preferences.

Extrovert/Introvert

The first area of difference looks at where people get their energy and how this impacts their relational patterns.

Extroverts derive energy from social contact, so they prefer to be with people most of the time. People interaction charges them up. Long stretches of aloneness weigh on them. Solitary work makes them feel "antsy." They need the stimulation of relationships, and they enjoy initiating and maintaining many of them. That's what keeps them fresh and vital.

Introverts derive energy from solitude, so they prefer to spend a lot of time alone. Quiet hours give them strength. If they spend too much time with people they become emotionally drained. It's not that they don't like people; it's just that they can't take heavy doses of them. They have to carefully balance their people interaction with lengthy blocks of solitude. They prefer a few significant relationships rather than many casual acquaintances.

If an introvert and an extrovert go on a private vacation together, after three or four days the introvert decides it would be great to live that way forever—in near-seclusion. At that point, the extrovert starts running from hotel room to hotel room, knocking on doors. "Hi! Hi! How long are you staying? Where are you from? Do you want to have lunch?"

Who's right? They both are.

Intuitive/Sensing

The second area of possible difference deals with how people take in and handle information, and how they solve problems.

Intuitive people focus on ideas and possibilities. They're imaginative people who constantly dream of better ways to do something, and ideas tend to pop full-blown into their heads during moments of inspiration. They are big-picture types who don't like to get mired down in intricate details and procedures. They see a problem, think about it awhile, then solve it according to gut-level perceptions. They just say, "Trust me, I know. I have a hunch about this. It's going to work out."

Sensing people say, "I'll trust you when I see the facts! Give me the pertinent data first." They are as sensible and realistic as the intuitives are imaginative, and accomplish more through perspiration than inspiration. They take in information through their senses—what they can see, hear, smell, or touch. They're very conscious of details, and more oriented to facts and figures than ideas and possibilities. They like charts and graphs and balance sheets, and meticulously follow their systems and procedures.

At our church board meetings I watch our board of directors wrestle with amazingly complex issues regarding the future of our church. They handle millions of dollars and make decisions that affect thousands of lives. The intuitors talk about the big picture, and come up with visionary plans for future growth and added ministries. The sensors reach for their calculators and start crunching numbers. They want to make sure the dreams are anchored in reality.

It's a good thing for our church that we have both kinds of leaders.

Thinkers/Feelers

The third area of differing preference has to do with how we make decisions.

Thinkers make decisions on the basis of clear logic and practicality. They take a cool, calculated approach and look at obvious cause and effect. If it makes sense, they do it. Clear and simple. Black and white. Thinkers are concerned about productivity, efficiency, profitability, effectiveness, and achievement of goals. If a thinking manager has to make a tough personnel decision, he decides what's right, then carries it out without trauma. He says, "Paul, you may hurt for a while, but you'll get over it. This is right for the company, and eventually you'll realize that it's best for you as well."

Feelers base their decisions on more people-oriented implications. They tune in to people's emotions and sentiments and ask, "How will this decision make them feel?" Because of this sensitivity, they agonize over confrontations and lose sleep over decisions that impact other people. They have a heightened ability to empathize. They are concerned with things like peace, harmony, and understanding.

When feelers see people in pain, they can actually feel the pain themselves. They have no trouble crying with those who cry. When thinkers see people in pain, they take a logical, unemotional approach. They determine the source of the problem or pain and suggest practical ways to alleviate it. Obviously the world needs both—people who can feel deeply and empathize, and people who can move ahead with practical solutions.

Structured/Unstructured[1]

This last category deals with basic life orientation.

Structured people prefer a predictable routine. They thrive on organization. They respond well to deadlines, rules, and policies. They like to make a plan and stick with it. They're frustrated by interruptions, surprises, or change. The fewer uncertainties there are in their lives, the happier they are. I call them "just-settle-it" people. They like it when the decisions are made, the plans are set, and everything's settled.

Unstructured people prefer spontaneity. They disdain routines, rules, and deadlines, and avoid planning at all costs. They prefer to let the day unfold naturally, and see what adventure might be just around the corner. They're unpredictable and oftentimes disorganized. I call them "play-it-by-ear" people, because they like life best when it's unplanned and unsettled, when all the options are open.

You can imagine the frustration that occurs when structured and unstructured people work or live together. They can drive each other crazy.

AH HA!

Lynne and I didn't have to read far to see why we had problems. Our "fundamental differences" were glaring.

We're both intuitives, so we didn't have to deal with "Intuitive/Sensing" conflicts. But in every other category we were extreme opposites. I'm an extrovert; Lynne's an introvert. I'm off the charts as a thinker; she's the ultimate feeler. I'm unstructured; she prefers structure.

As we looked back over the years, we realized we had some heavy duty apologizing to do.

For years I had tried to get Lynne to be more relational, not realizing that God made her to thrive in an environment rich in solitude. He gave her gifts, abilities, and talents that need to be nurtured in quiet aloneness. Because I didn't understand that, I pushed her into a lifestyle that depleted her energy and left her empty. And then I wondered why she was frustrated, unhappy, and unproductive.

During those same years Lynne questioned my love for her because of what she considered my extreme involvement with friends and colleagues. She assumed I found her boring or undesirable. Why else would I crave so many outside relationships? She made me feel guilty for my sociability, and then wondered why I felt stifled and trapped.

Now we do everything possible to free one another to be who God made us to be. I free Lynne to live a quieter, more solitary life. She frees me to enjoy the level of relationality I naturally desire.

What a difference that's made! Lynne has blossomed as a woman, wife, mother, and servant of Christ as she's pursued a quieter life. At the end of a day I love hearing about the work she's accomplished, the book she's read, or the insights she's gained during her solitary hours.

As I've pursued and nurtured a multitude of relationships, I've been stretched and challenged to become a better man. In the end that's enhanced my relationship with Lynne. She brings to our relationship the strength of her solitude, and I bring the stimulation of my interactions. The same differences that used to hinder our relationship now enhance it. What we tried so hard to change, we now cherish.

The same is true in the thinking/feeling area. For years Lynne accused me of being heartless and cruel because I so easily made tough decisions that made people uncomfortable or upset. I thought she was neurotic and mushy because she was so unrealistically concerned about how people felt and what they thought.

Yet we each have a perspective that our world, church, family, and relationship desperately needs. My tough decision making has to be softened by Lynne's sensitivity. Her empathy has to be balanced by my practicality.

What about the structured/unstructured conflict? It's the same old story. For years we locked horns. She was frustrated by my unpredictability, and I was impatient with her planning. But once we understood our fundamental difference, we could work around it.

Now I make it a point to alert Lynne to changes or new ideas as soon as possible so she can have time to plan and prepare. And I've come to appreciate her organizational abilities. Our family life would be chaos if she didn't keep me and the kids in order.

At the same time, Lynne has learned to be more flexible and accept my spontaneity. And she's learned that it's okay to set aside the schedule now and then and "play it by ear." It can even be fun.

Once again, our differences have become benefits. I provide the adventure; she provides the plan that makes the adventure work.

Do you see how important it is to understand these fundamental temperament differences? It's hard to love someone authentically when you don't understand them. It's hard to resolve conflicts when you can't see the underlying issues. Lynne and I could have avoided years of frustration if we had realized that we weren't better or worse than one another—just different. When you accept and quit passing moral judgment on those differences, you open the door for workable compromise. You end up delighting in the very differences that once caused division.

What about you? Do you and your spouse need to patiently understand each other's ways of behaving that stem from different inborn temperament traits? Then do it! Or better yet, find a counselor who can give you the Myers-Briggs Type Indicator test, and help you work through the results. It's an investment that could revolutionize the most important relationship in your life.

YOU GOTTA SAY IT RIGHT

The second key to establishing authenticity in marriage is learning the appropriate language of love.

Several years ago I met a man at a social function at our church. During our conversation, he repeatedly referred to how much he loved and appreciated his wife. He told me how much he delighted in her presence and how easy it was to tell her he loved her. I reflected later that it was refreshing to meet a man so enthused about his marriage.

A short time later, this man's wife came to me for counseling. Her problem was her relationship with her husband. She was convinced he didn't love her. I couldn't believe it!

After several sessions with the husband and wife together, guess what I learned? The husband really was in love with his wife; he had not lied to me. But I also learned that the wife really did not feel loved. For some reason, her husband's expressions of love were not doing the job.

I didn't understand why they had this problem. If he loved her, why couldn't she feel it? I've learned since then that the husband was simply not speaking the right language. He was expressing love, but not in terms his wife could understand.

Just as we have inborn preferences regarding relational patterns, problem solving, decision making, and structure, so we have preferences in regard to giving and receiving love. Most of us aren't aware of this, but it's true. We each prefer certain "languages" of love.

Here are some of the common ones.

Touch. Some people just naturally touch the people they love. If they want to tell someone they love them, they kiss their cheek, or hold their hand, or gather them up in a bear hug. That's what comes naturally to them.

Verbal expression. When these people feel love welling up within them, their only comfortable outlet is their mouth. "I love you. I love you." While some people find it hard to express their love in words, these people can't stop.

Service. These people communicate love by serving the beloved.

For them, love isn't love unless it's demonstrated in practical terms—wallpapering the kitchen, washing the car, preparing favorite meals.

Providers. These people consider their breadwinning to be the greatest expression of their love. Providers go to great lengths to ensure that even after they're gone, their loved ones will be well-provided for.

Gift-givers. These people keep the department stores solvent. They love to buy little gifts (or big ones), wrap them beautifully, and present them with childish glee to the ones they love.

Opportunity enthusiasts. These people like to think of ways to challenge and inspire their loved ones to greatness. Their goal is to open up opportunities that will offer stimulation and fulfillment.

Time-givers. These people are primarily concerned with fellowship. They're willing to rearrange their schedules so they can offer large blocks of time to the significant people in their lives.

As you go down this list, can you pick out your preferred language of love? Can you pick out your spouse's? Do you both speak the same language?

A CLEAN MISS

For years Lynne and I spoke different languages of love and didn't even know it.

Lynne decided early in our marriage that to communicate love to me, she needed to speak the language of the Galloping Gourmet. She knocked herself out every evening to prepare lovely meals that she thought would make me feel loved. They didn't. I'm not a connoisseur of fine foods, and a gourmet meal says the same thing to me as a tuna sandwich.

I finally told her that. I said, "Don't spend all this time on fancy meals. It doesn't matter to me. Just sit down and talk to me. Tell me I'm great. Call me a super-husband. Encourage me. Cheer me on. That'll make me feel loved."

Being an introvert, Lynne is not naturally free with words. But when she learned I needed to hear love, she disciplined herself to become more verbally expressive. To put it bluntly, she learned to tell me what I needed to hear. Sometimes she even writes little notes and sticks them on my mirror, so I can start the day with her words of affirmation.

Another way I enjoy receiving love is through having people open doors of opportunity for me. Because I appreciate this, I assumed Lynne would, too. For years I did everything in my power to offer opportunities that would stimulate and inspire her. I urged her to take flying lessons, or skydiving lessons, or go helicopter skiing in the Rocky Mountains. What an encourager I was.

Finally she said, "Bill, why are you always pushing me? I feel like you're never satisfied with what I'm doing. You're always trying to head me off in new directions. I wish that once in a while you would just put your arms around me, hold me, and let me feel loved and accepted just the way I am."

I was shocked. I thought I was doing her a favor, and in reality I was making her feel pressured and inadequate. What she really needed was a loving embrace, but that honestly never crossed my mind.

Do you see how important it is for spouses to understand and communicate their preferences for receiving love? Most of us mistakenly assume our spouses want to receive love the same way we do. So whatever language comes most naturally to us, we use with them. That usually doesn't work.

We must tell one another which love language communicates most clearly to us. It's not hard to learn new ways of communicating love. And it can transform a marriage where spouses *hope* they're loved into a marriage where they *know* they are.

Here's a personal challenge. Look over the seven languages of love I described, and decide which you prefer to give and receive. Have your spouse do the same. Then go out for dinner and discuss your findings. If this helps you as much as it did Lynne and me, you'll be on the road to a more loving marriage—immediately.

LET'S HAVE FUN!

One afternoon, shortly after we were married, Lynne and I heard a noisy commotion in our front yard. We ran out and found a big, custom-painted Harley Davidson motorcycle with two riders in black leather jackets and big black helmets with tinted visors that covered their faces. They had driven right up on our sidewalk, and the driver was revving the engine as high as possible. Finally, the rider on the back slid off, removed her helmet—and it was Lynne's mother!

Here was my demure mother-in-law, and my hardworking father-in-law sitting on a motorcycle in the middle of my sidewalk! They had ridden over from Michigan to surprise us.

I was shocked. I was speechless.

Finally Lynne said, "Relax, Bill. It's no big deal. They do things like this all the time."

For years I had been impressed with Lynne's parents' marriage. It was so obvious that after decades of marriage they were still madly in love with one another. Finally I learned the secret of their success: "They do things like this all the time."

That was it. They had learned to have fun together, to break out of the routine, to be friends and lovers again. When you do that on a regular basis, it's almost impossible for a marriage to go bad.

One of the major reasons for marital breakdown is plain old-fashioned boredom. A couple establishes a routine—they do their work, handle family business, fulfill social obligations, watch TV—and before they know what's happening their relationship goes stale.

Maybe they don't scream and yell and fight. But neither do they enjoy the "ecstasies of marital bliss." They talk now and then, but they're certainly not soul mates. They go through the motions of sex, but even that's more routine than it is romantic.

How can we avoid that pattern? Here are four ideas:

1. Lynne and I decided to begin by becoming religiously devoted to our weekly date. Every Thursday morning we go out for a long breakfast and "catch up" on one another's lives.

We relate anecdotes about our week and discuss decisions or family plans we have to make. Sometimes we talk about books we've both read. Occasionally we spend the morning in the tunnel of chaos, working through conflicts that have risen since our last meeting. That's not fun, but it keeps molehills from growing into mountains, and frees us to enjoy one another again.

If you were to ask either of us to name our favorite time of the week, we'd say Thursday morning. We need that time to pull ourselves out of our busy schedules, drop the responsibilities of work and family life, and just be Bill and Lynne, out on a date like we were twenty years ago.

Why a breakfast date instead of a candlelight dinner? We're both morning people and want to give each other the best time of our day. If you're night people, go for dinner. If you're one of each, split the difference and go for high tea. What's important is that you find a workable time and stick with it.

2. We've made it a point to develop common fun interests. Though most people wouldn't consider "running" a fun activity, we've

found that it is when we do it together. Often when the weather's nice we run together when I get home from work. We also enjoy nature and found a beautiful, secluded area not far from home where we can take long, quiet walks. When we're in a more rambunctious mood, we ride trail bikes at a friend's farm. In the summer we swim, windsurf, and pursue our favorite leisure activity—sailing.

Why is it so important to do things like this? Because when we're having fun with one another we see each other in a new light. We recapture the feeling of youthfulness and vitality we had when we first met. We joke and laugh and break down inhibitions. We create an aura of warmth and love and closeness.

3. We make frequent use of overnight getaways and vacations. Everything that is accomplished on a weekly date is multiplied during extended times away. For years Lynne and I were careless and sporadic about this. We were so busy with ministry and kids that it seemed impossible to get away.

But when we started seeing Christian leaders all around us shipwrecking their marriages, we decided we had to do something to keep that from happening. So we committed ourselves to taking periodic breaks for relaxation, refreshment, and fun.

Every time we return from a trip, whether we've been gone for two days or two weeks, we're amazed anew at the progress we've made in our relationship and the closeness we feel.

4. We've made a mutual commitment to make our sexual relationship everything it was meant to be. When we got married, we committed ourselves to sexual fidelity. We said, "All our sexual hopes and expectations we give to one another. We will never seek to satisfy them elsewhere."

That means that if Lynne is ever going to be swept off her feet by a knight in shining armor, I'm going to have to do the sweeping. And if I'm ever going to have my sexual dreams come true, Lynne's going to have to make them happen. We believe we owe it to one another to do everything we can to fulfill one another's sexual needs.

In theory, of course, that sounds easy. In reality, it's a tall order. At least it was for us.

The chronic overscheduling in the early years of our marriage, and the unresolved tensions that existed because we weren't willing to face our tunnel of chaos, created hostility that made meaningful lovemaking impossible.

So our commitment to sexual satisfaction meant we had to go back to the beginning and work through the issues that had created the hostility. Only then were we free to experience and express genuine feelings of love.

We also had to learn that mutually satisfying sex doesn't begin in the bedroom. It begins in the restaurant where we meet for breakfast, in the kitchen where we stop for a brief conversation before the kids come in for dinner, in the backyard where we sit in lawn chairs and talk over the day.

When men complain to me that their wives aren't interested in their sexual relationship, I often ask what kind of communication patterns exist in their marriage. Do they enjoy meaningful conversations with their wives on a regular basis? There's an undeniable tie between conversational intimacy and physical intimacy.

Another key to sexual fulfillment relates to the previous point in this chapter: learning the language of love. Someone who genuinely feels loved is much more enthusiastic about lovemaking than someone who doesn't. For many people, sexuality is deeply tied to emotional and psychological realities.

Achieving mutually satisfying sex is no simple matter. But it's worth all the time, effort, and creativity it demands. At one time sex was the greatest frustration in our marriage. Now it provides the greatest fun.

What is an authentic marriage? It's a marriage where differences are seen as blessings. Where spouses really feel loved. And where routine gives way to conversation, fun, and romance.

For some people it seems like a far-off dream. But it's not an impossible goal. Why not renew your commitment to building the kind of marriage God wants you to enjoy.

NOTES

1. Keirsey and Bates call this last category "Judging vs. Perceiving." In choosing to call it "Structured vs. Unstructured," I have undoubtedly over-simplified a very complex distinction. These terms, however, seemed to help my congregation grasp the essence of the authors' meaning.

7

Raising Image-bearers: The High Call of Parenting

In the 1940s, the top offenses committed by public school students were talking, chewing gum, making noises, running in the halls, getting out of turn in line, wearing improper clothing, and not putting paper in the wastebasket.

In 1982, the top offenses had changed. They had become rape, robbery, assault, burglary, arson, bombing, murder, and suicide.[1]

The behavior of children changed dramatically in the forty years separating those findings. Why? "Today's teenagers live in a different world from the one you remember. The nuclear family has exploded. Dr. Spock has given way to Dr. Ruth. A million hours of television have made kids talk like valley girls, dress like rock stars, and think like game show contestants."[2]

THE EXPLODED FAMILY

That writer emphasized one reason for the drastic changes we see in children today—the fragmented family. In my high school graduating class of 1970, there was not one student from a single-parent family. Today's projections indicate that two out of three white children between birth and age eighteen will spend at least part of their growing-up years in a single-parent family. In the black community, nineteen out of twenty children are expected to do so.[3] The statistics are staggering—and so are the effects.

Several years ago, the University of California tested fifth and sixth graders to determine what caused them the highest degree of sadness, anxiety, and depression. The top answers? Having parents separate or divorce, having parents argue with one another, and having parents who didn't spend enough time with them.[4]

Time magazine reported the findings of a recent study measuring the long-term effects of growing up in a fragmented family. The *Time* article concluded that close to half of the children from families broken by divorce go into adulthood as men and women who worry, are underachievers, have poor self-images, and often are very angry.

> Two-thirds of the girls, many of whom had seemingly sailed through the crisis of divorce, suddenly became deeply anxious as young adults, unable to make lasting commitments and fearful of betrayal in intimate relationships. Many boys, who were more overtly troubled in the postdivorce years, failed to develop a sense of independence, confidence or purpose. They drifted in and out of college and from job to job.[5]

That's sobering information. And the current divorce rate of over fifty percent means that every year thousands more children enter that milieu of brokenness. No wonder nearly eighty percent of students say at the end of high school that a happy and successful marriage is one of the most important goals in life.[6]

PUSHY PARENTS

Another reason for the changing behavior of children is the increased pressure imposed by overachieving parents.

In the movie *Baby Boom* Diane Keaton feels like an outcast because she has not yet enrolled her two-year-old daughter in a music appreciation class. "She'll have so much catching up to do," quips another mother.

A first-grade teacher told the story of an irate mother who screamed at her because she had given her son a "satisfactory" on his report card. "How is he ever going to get into M.I.T. if you give him a 'Satisfactory'!" she wailed.[7]

It's a "toddler-eat-toddler" world out there, as a new generation of children called "Yuppie Puppies" compete for the honor roll in preschool classes. One child-development expert sees many eight-year-olds suffering from acute anxiety, and nine- and ten-year-olds having lost all sense of what it means to be a child.[8]

MEDIA MODELS

A third reason for changing childhood behavior is the role models children are exposed to today.

When I was growing up, Ricky Nelson and Wally Cleaver were the role models. Eddie Haskell was the closest thing to an antihero I knew. My mother warned me never to hang around with guys like him.

But times have changed. Today television, videos, and movies bombard young people with media models who say, sing, and do the unimaginable. Madonna's album, *Like a Prayer,* is more concerned with exorcizing demons than entertaining fans. The heavy metal group "Guns and Roses" produced an album called *Appetite for Destruction.* The back cover gruesomely pictures a woman recently raped and knifed.

What young people see on MTV, home videos, and the hot new horror films—slice-and-dice flicks—would make most parents vomit. Eddie Haskell looks like an altar boy compared to current media characters.

AN UNDENIABLE CRISIS

Numerous other factors negatively influence children's behavior. There's the problem of peer pressure to use drugs and alcohol. The National Adolescent Student Health Survey published by the Center for Disease Control showed that seventy-seven percent of eighth graders surveyed had tried alcohol. By tenth grade the figure had grown to eighty-nine percent of those surveyed.[9] Drug use is reaching an equally alarming percentage—as high as fifty percent, some say. Addiction is becoming a common problem.

There's also pornography, which is being aimed at a younger and younger audience every year. And the pressure to be sexually promiscuous. In my son's fourth grade class, boys taunted one another to "have sex" with nine-year-old girls.

There are the free-floating anxieties caused by nuclear threat,

economic and environmental instability, and AIDS. There's fear
aroused by increased sexual abuse and domestic violence.

On top of all this, there's the hopelessness most kids feel when
they seek spiritual assistance from a church that's locked in the Middle
Ages and refuses to acknowledge the changing world around it.

The combination of these pressures is tearing the soul out of a
whole generation of young people. The suicide rate for teenagers has
tripled in the last twenty years. Nearly four hundred thousand teens
attempt suicide each year, and about six thousand succeed.[10] In the
survey by the Centers for Disease Control, more than one-third
(thirty-four percent) of the eighth and tenth graders surveyed had
seriously considered taking their own lives.[11]

If I'd given a message on suicide when I was in youth work in the
early seventies, the kids would have wondered why. Today, when the
junior high director at our church gives such a message, the kids are all
ears. It's a subject that touches all of them.

Concerned Christians have to address these changes and determine ways to reverse these depressing trends. Those of us with
children must learn to parent authentically, instilling in our children
the strength, integrity, and values that will help them stand firm in a
changing world. In this chapter I want to give several suggestions for
doing that.

START WITH STABILITY

First, newly married couples should devote themselves to solidify-
ing their marriage before they even consider having children.

Conventional wisdom says: Finish high school. Go to college. Get
married and start a family. Don't ask questions. Just use standard
operating procedure.

Unfortunately, conventional wisdom underestimates the stress
and struggle of the early years of marriage. It ignores the fact that
nearly thirty-four percent of divorces occur within four years of the
wedding.[12]

Jesus tells us to be "as shrewd as snakes and as innocent as doves"
(Matt. 10:16). I think that means that sometimes we have to challenge
conventional wisdom. I think it means that before young couples
consider parenthood, they need to consider the requirements for a
stable marriage. They need to realize how much time it takes to
develop communication skills and the ability to solve conflicts and

build the security that leads to intimacy. Young couples need to consider the effort it takes to establish a well-functioning household and a workable financial plan. It takes time and effort to get on track spiritually and sort out values and priorities. Finally it takes time to establish a network of like-minded couples to provide support, encouragement, and wisdom.

This may sound like overly extensive and unnecessary ground-work. But with fragmented families killing our society—and our children—can we afford to do less? Young couples need to take all the steps to build stable marriages *before* they think about having children. Raising a healthy, well-adjusted, Christ-honoring child in today's world almost demands a strong marriage and family unit.

TO HAVE OR NOT TO HAVE

As a second step to authentic parenting, married couples should seek God's wisdom about whether or not to have children. This applies even to firmly established married couples.

That almost sounds like heresy, doesn't it? Most of us have heard the command to "Be fruitful and multiply" all our lives. We've never considered "not being fruitful" as a legitimate option.

But few contemporary biblical scholars believe God's command to Adam and Eve to populate the earth implies a similar command to every potential childbearer today. Mankind has done a magnificent job of multiplying; the earth is well-populated. This commandment provides no obvious basis for assuming that God wants all couples to have children. God is more than able to give married couples personalized guidance on this very important decision.

A Painful Past

Over the years I've noted several kinds of situations in which God might lead a couple not to start a family. The first is where one or both marriage partners carries the deep trauma of a painful or tragic past. Many young adults today come from fragmented, dysfunctional, or abusive families. Many were raised by parents who were unable to provide love and understanding or who were afflicted by alcoholism or drug addiction. The unpleasant truth is that it may take those young people years to process the resulting painful memories and establish emotional wholeness.

Young couples scarred with painful pasts may be able to build solid marriages, but in some cases, the addition of a wild-card pressure—like a child—would be enough to tip the delicate emotional balance. Such couples should question the wisdom of risking their emotional and marital stability to start a family.

They should also examine the implications of passing their debilitations to another generation. During nearly two decades in ministry, I have seen plenty of "generational baton passing." Too often it's been a tragic transfer. Time and again I've seen young people from dysfunctional families get married and have children without first working through their emotional brokenness. What happens? They pass to their children the same baton of pain they received.

I want to shout, "When will this *stop*? When will people quit passing broken batons? When will they slow down long enough to establish patterns of health?" It's not fair to load down innocent children with the complications their parents should have taken care of before they had children.

God is capable of helping newly married couples work through the pains of the past. But He's also capable of determining that, in some situations, childbearing would be ill-advised. In the best interests of the would-be parents and the possible offspring, He might lead a couple not to pursue parenthood.

A Legitimate Choice

God might also guide a married couple to forego having children if both partners are highly motivated to pursue full-time careers, either in the ministry or in the marketplace.

In our church, hundreds of godly young couples are totally at peace with their decision to pursue career rather than family. Many have proven to be effective missionaries in the marketplace, using their platform of achievement to call coworkers and friends to Jesus Christ. Others have devoted their talents and gifts to full-time ministry, accomplishing significant work both in our church and the church at large.

For years couples who chose career rather than family have been called selfish and immature, because they've appeared unwilling to sacrifice the perks of the marketplace for the selflessness of parenting. In some cases, that may be true. For many couples, however, the choice is valid, well-thought-out, and truly God-honoring.

Conflict of Interests

There is, however, cause for concern—major concern—when young couples make their primary commitment to their careers, and then choose to have children "on the side." These couples apparently want to "have" children, but seem unwilling to "raise" them.

There's little mystery about how children are conceived and delivered. But many two-career couples seem to be remarkably naive about what it takes to parent them. They seem to think kids raise themselves.

Raising children is an enormously demanding challenge. So demanding, in fact, that God clearly assigns *both* parents to carry it out. In Ephesians 6 and Colossians 3, Paul addresses his comments on parenting to both parents. His plural noun makes mothers and fathers equally responsible for raising, training, nurturing, and disciplining their children. He does that not to free them to share equal *irresponsibility*, as some parents seem to assume, but to challenge them to share equal *responsibility*.

This may detonate a few land mines, but parents, I have to remind you that nannies, baby-sitters, relatives, and day-care workers will never give an ultimate account to God for how they raised your children. You will give that account. You will. And Lynne and I will give an account for how we raise our children. That's sobering, isn't it?

I regularly talk with expectant married couples who are clearly annoyed that the baby is going to make the mother miss six weeks of work. "Right during the busiest season of the year!" The father, of course, won't interrupt his climb up the ladder, so they face a dilemma. Who'll take care of the baby? Repeatedly I'm asked if I know a church member who can babysit from 7:00 A.M. to 6:00 P.M., five days a week, and sometimes on weekends.

I'm tempted to print bumper stickers that say, *Parents, do you know who is raising your children?* The mindset is fast becoming: We'll make them; you raise them. I cringe when I detect that attitude, and I believe God cries.

I'm not directing these comments at single parents. Most single parents have no option but to work full-time to support themselves and their children. For them, child care is a means of survival. The weight of responsibility they carry is immense, and for too long Christians have condemned their plight without offering assistance. In recent years the church has launched numerous ministries to lighten the load for single parents, and I believe it must do even more.

However, it's a different story for couples who like the idea of having children, but are looking for low-demand methods for raising them. They have to realize that low-demand methods aren't realistic. You can't microwave children from the embryonic state into immediate adulthood. It takes time and energy to raise children. Young couples hoping to find a system of child-rearing that doesn't inconvenience them or overload their already full schedules should rethink their decision. It may be they're missing the whole point of having children.

IMAGE-BEARERS

God created Adam and Eve in His own image and pronounced them "Very Good!" Then He commanded them to make additional reproductions of His image through procreation.

During his 1988 presidential campaign, George Bush talked about "a thousand points of light." That phrase captures God's idea of millions of pure reflections of His glory, illuminating every dark corner of the world, radiating hope and life. Adam and Eve's multiplied offspring were to brighten the world by mirroring the greatness of God's character and power.

Most Christians have lost sight of that truth. They've forgotten, or never knew, that the primary reason for having children is to raise shining, active, young image-bearers who are motivated and trained to carry the torch of authentic Christianity into the next generation.

True followers of Jesus Christ don't have children merely for the fellowship factor. Or so they can pass on property and the family name. Or to avoid loneliness in their later years. They view parenting as the opportunity to invest themselves fully in the life of a child who will someday become an irresistible manifestation of God's grace and make a difference by exercising his or her unique talents and gifts. That's our motivation for bearing and raising children—and our challenge.

Sin complicated this challenge. Adam and Eve's disobedience stained not only themselves, but their lineage as well. From that day on, parents would birth children who had the *potential* to reflect God's glory; but drawing that potential out would require great amounts of parental leadership, love, energy, interaction, discipline, and prayer.

Christian parents who truly understand the goal of parenting—to draw out the image-bearing potential of each child—become fully engaged in the challenge. They no longer just build businesses. They build character, value, and vision into young lives. They no longer treat their children as inconveniences to be handed off to anyone who will tend them for five dollars an hour. These parents see the "season of parenting" as the ultimate spiritual challenge, worthy of their best efforts, most fervent prayers, and largest investments of time. They search for ways to improve their skills through books, tapes, seminars, and interacting with other parents. These parents look to the church for assistance, and they support with their time, money, and prayer, the ministries that enhance their children's spiritual training.

In short, they do *anything* they can to encourage authentic Christian growth in their children—even if it slows their professional advancement and postpones the pursuit of personal dreams. They know that molding a runny-nosed little bandit into a God-honoring difference-maker is the most stretching, demanding, and, ultimately, fulfilling challenge they can face. So they earnestly devote themselves to it.

WHAT REALLY MATTERS

Recently I talked to a young father in our church parking lot. While he wired the bumper onto his car, he said, "I have to admit it's embarrassing to drive a car that's literally falling apart, but I've got a good reason. My wife and I are committed to staying out of debt so we don't financially strangle our family. We want to have fun family experiences. We want to travel together. We want to send our kids to Christian camps. If we drove a late-model car, we couldn't afford those things. So we made our choice."

Another father, employed by a Christian organization, was asked how he was going to afford college educations for his four children. "Simple," he said. "My wife and I are going to sell our home, and use the equity to put our kids through a Christian college." Their plan was to move into a mobile home or an inexpensive apartment. "It doesn't really matter where we end up living. What matters is that our children end up in an environment that can stimulate their spiritual growth. We want them to become spiritual champions." That's the kind of attitude parents have when they understand the goal of parenting.

As my brother and I approached junior high school, our dad

became concerned that we would find the church youth group boring and lose interest in spiritual concerns. So he bought an old Greyhound bus, tore the seats out, and installed a small kitchen and some bunk beds. With two other fathers, he took the boys in the youth group on trips to places like Niagara Falls, Mackinac Island, and Mammoth Cave. None of the men could cook, so the food was terrible. And none knew how to teach Bible studies, so our formal training was nonexistent. But what memories!

I knew, even as a little guy, that Dad was busy and had many people tugging at his time. I knew he could have been doing deals instead of driving a Greyhound bus around the Midwest with ten rebellious, junior high boys. But he was determined to transform what could have been a discouraging era in our spiritual formation into an adventure. He knew his goal: to produce difference-makers, spiritual champions, children who could grow up to be impact players for the cause of Christ.

My dad was an eccentric man who did unconventional things to keep us kids from straying off the path. Some people even thought he went overboard. But from his vantage point in heaven, I bet he's eternally glad he did!

NO REGRETS

I've made no secret of the fact that early in my ministry I was so overscheduled that I would often go two or three weeks without being home a single night with my family. During that time I began reading biographies of some of the great Christian leaders. Frequently, near the end of the books, the biographers recorded the leaders' answers to the question: If you could live your life over again, would you do anything differently? Almost always the response was, "I built a great ministry, but I broke the hearts of my children. I served others at their expense. I embittered them against God and against me. If I could do it over again, I'd properly balance ministry and family."

Those words, and the personal confrontations of friends who saw the course I was on, challenged me to change my schedule. I accepted the challenge and vowed I would never make my children pay for my involvement in ministry. By God's grace, and thanks to Lynne and the men in my accountability group, I have maintained that commitment.

But what if I had been challenged too late in life? Or if I had neglected the challenge? Some of us don't have the luxury of doing better the second time around because of the shortness and uncertainty of life. Will there be regrets?

Several years ago a close friend of mine lost his only child, a twenty-four-year-old son, in a drowning accident. Shortly after the accident, I heard a tape of an interview in which his wife was asked how she coped with the death of her only child. She said, "I can live with the loss of my child because I can honestly say that I have no regrets about how I raised him. I wasn't a perfect mother, of course. But I poured time and energy and love into him from the day he was born. I have no regrets about that."

I can still remember where I was, driving down the road toward my house, when I heard those words. I squeezed the steering wheel and said, "God, that's my commitment from this day forward! I want to live every day without regret regarding my children. I want to pour everything I can into them during the short season that I have them."

A DAILY STRUGGLE

Usually I go to my office for a few hours on Saturday morning to "tweak" the final draft of my weekend message. One Saturday when I was finishing a message on this subject of parenting, Lynne was out of town and Shauna was visiting a friend, so Todd was home alone. He usually doesn't mind that, but that morning was different. Within one hour, he called me three times: "Dad, you done yet?" The third time he called, my heart sank and I thought, "Here I am trying to tweak a message encouraging parents to build into their kids, and I have a little boy at home desperately needing to be 'built into.' What am I doing?" I went home, and that weekend I gave an adequate, but definitely untweaked message.

What's my point? That it's a struggle. That I still wrestle every day with difficult choices. That sometimes we have to give up something good for the sake of something better. My schedule gets more complicated every year, but I am committed to doing everything in my power to attend soccer games and recitals, to plan family vacations, to tuck my kids into bed at night, to pray around the dinner table, and to do whatever I can to build into my kids during the few years I have them.

My goal isn't just to keep them from being an embarrassment to me. Or to help them grow up well-adjusted so they can live the All-American Dream. My goal is for them to become bright reflections of the image of God, radiating hope and life to a dreary, wicked world. That goal is worthy of my most prodigious efforts.

IMPART LIFE

Authentic parenting involves more than giving birth. It demands that we truly impart life—emotional and spiritual as well as physical. The catch is that we can't impart what we don't have. We can't pass on emotional well-being if we've not grown beyond the deficiencies of our own emotional history. We can't pass on spiritual vitality unless we've nurtured a personal faith that is life-changing and empowering.

Are you contemplating parenthood? Please, don't rush into it. Examine yourself. Be honest about your emotional and spiritual maturity. Pray to determine God's specific direction for you in this most important decision.

Are you a parent? Then remind yourself of your goal. Devote yourself to your task. Make the tough choices. Determine to live without regrets regarding your children.

Are you a pastor or church leader? Then get behind your ministries to youth, family, and single parents. Be willing to pour time, money, staff, and creativity into programs to make a difference in your children's lives. Your church nursery and classrooms are filled with little image-bearers whose potential must be lovingly and wisely drawn out.

Never before have children faced greater pressures. Never before have societal forces so conflicted with godly goals. Never before has the need for tenacious, courageous, fully engaged parenting been so great.

NOTES

1. *Indianapolis Tech Challenge Newsletter* (January 1983).
2. Randy Peterson, "Youth or Consequences: We Can't Ignore Teens," *Christian Retailing* 35, no. 4 (April 15, 1989), 1.
3. The Rand Institute Study, in "Richard Russell's Dow Theory Letters" (March 22, 1989), 5.
4. Beth Weinhouse, "How To Raise a Happy, Healthy Child: Kids And Stress," *Ladies' Home Journal* 105, no. 8 (August 1988), 58.
5. Written by Anastasia Toufexis, reported by Georgia Harbison/New York, "The Lasting Wounds of Divorce," *Time* 133, no. 6 (February 6, 1989), 61.
6. Selina S. Guber, "The Teenage Mind," *American Demographics* (August 1987), 43.
7. David Eklind, "Superkids and Super Problems," *Psychology Today* (May 1987), 60.

8. Kim M. Magon, "Toddlers Find World Is Tough," *Pulitzer Lerner Community Newspapers*, 9.
9. "One in Three Teens Considered Suicide, Survey Finds," *Chicago Tribune* (March 10, 1989), 16.
10. Tom Naughton, "Growing Pains, Growing Pressures," *Family Safety and Health* (Spring 1987), 26.
11. "One in Three Teens," 16.
12. Illinois Department of Public Health, "Vital Statistics, Illinois, 1987" (April 1989), I:01.

8

Honest Emotions

She was young, attractive, gifted—a devoted wife and mother and a faithful leader in the church. Then her world fell apart. An inexplicable anxiety suddenly became debilitating. She ended up in the psychiatric ward of a local hospital. Months of intense therapy uncovered the horror of childhood sexual abuse. In a complex and desperate attempt to protect her from the pain of reality, her mind had covered up the truth for years. But now the cover-up was cracking, the truth was oozing out, and the pain was too great to bear.

He was a successful businessman, a beloved father and grand-father, a warm friend, a devout Christian. His only problem was his uncontrolled eating. Diets and exercise programs helped for a while but always ended in defeat. His excess weight led to discouragement and heart trouble. Finally, a counselor showed him the connection between his compulsive eating habits and the emotional abuse he had experienced in the home of a harsh and insensitive father.

She was the tough, aggressive type: unemotional and indepen-dent, confident and self-assured, competent in business and relation-ships. Sure, there had been disappointments, but they hadn't gotten her down. She suffered none of the usual effects of growing up in a broken home. She had faced job loss, miscarriage, and relational disappointments with calm resignation. She was on top of things. Until the tears hit. With no warning, the dam broke. Years of unacknowledged grief consolidated into an overwhelming flood of tears. She thought she had successfully avoided the pain. But in the end, the pain won.

Psychologists would tell us that these people are dealing with "unfinished business"—issues from the past that negatively affect their present behavior because they never properly dealt with the problems. Pain that was submerged. Fear that was denied. Feelings of loss and grief that were ignored. The experts tell us that unfinished business is the source of many of the emotional and relational difficulties we face.

For years the Christian community has disagreed. For the most part, the church has been unwilling to believe that psychological concepts like "unfinished business" have any legitimate relationship to the difficulties Christians face. According to the church, the problem is sin, and the solution is repentance. The key to success, happiness, and overcoming pain is to get your mind off yourself and on to the Lord.

Get involved with worship.

Devote yourself to praise.

Defeat the Evil One.

Don't dredge up the past. Don't look inside. Don't walk around with a sad face. As the great apostle Paul said, "Rejoice in the Lord always. I will say it again: Rejoice!" (Phil. 4:4). Is this the road to an authentic emotional life for a Christian?

CONFUSION REIGNS

Verses like Philippians 4:4—and there are plenty of them in Scripture—have caused tremendous confusion in the body of Christ. More than once I've stood by the side of a believer who's mourning the loss of a loved one and overheard something like this: "Well Mary, we're praising the Lord with you today. Harold is home with his heavenly Father. He's rejoicing right now with us. Isn't it wonderful to be able to praise God even in this? You are praising God, aren't you, Mary? You're not losing the victory, are you?" Mary mumbles her thanks, then inwardly chastises herself for not being a stronger Christian. Why can't she sing the "Hallelujah Chorus" at her husband's funeral like she's supposed to?

I mean, isn't that what Philippians 4:4 tells her to do? Doesn't it tell her—and us—to rejoice over death, loss, injury, trial, failure, and defeat? Doesn't it tell the elders of our church, who regularly pray with seriously afflicted people, to rejoice over eyes that don't see, limbs that don't function, wombs that are barren, or hearts that are broken? Doesn't it tell them to meet with the grieving and trembling, the broken and beaten down, and chastise them for not "rejoicing always"?

It does seem to say that. Paul says, "Rejoice in the Lord always; and if you have any confusion about that, let me say it again, rejoice!" So, many Christians decide to rejoice no matter what—even if that means denying their pain, loss, anger, embarrassment, hurt, or feelings of abandonment. Even if they have to bury their unfinished business one more time. They've been taught that the Christian cure for grief is to spiritualize it away. If they praise God passionately enough, the full effect of the tragedy will never take hold. It's like a Teflon shield. Just pray, and the grief will slide right off.

Some Christians make heroes of people who smile and sing their way through funerals of loved ones. They make role models of those who never crack, never cry, never stop praising God in the midst of the deepest valleys. If only other Christians would be like them. If they would just listen to more messages, memorize more verses, and fill their minds with more Christian music, they too could submerge the pain and "Praise the Lord Anyway!"

But in your heart of hearts don't you sometimes wonder? Is all that rejoicing real? Or does denial play a role? Are valid emotions being submerged? Are pain and anger and hurt being stuffed into a vault that's going to explode someday?

I have actually heard sincere, godly women say things like this: "Bill, just last night I found out that my husband's been unfaithful. But it's okay. I'm sure God has a better plan. He's going to work this out. My husband may not be faithful, but God is. With your help, the elders' prayers, and my friends' support, I'm going to be fine."

Such a controlled response in a situation like that makes me uneasy. I want to shake those women and say, "Dear friend, it's all right for you to be so mad right now that you can't talk straight. It's all right for you to feel so violated you want to fall in a pile and cry until someone picks you up. It's okay to feel that way and to admit those feelings." I get very uncomfortable when Christians try to prove their maturity and love for God by refusing to acknowledge legitimate pain. I fear they're not being authentic in regard to their emotions.

But then there's the other extreme. Some people don't believe at all in this opium called rejoicing. They can't find anything praiseworthy in pain. In fact, they leave God out of the picture entirely. Their counsel is to just feel the full force of whatever pain is coming our way. "Own your anger," they say. "Explore your violated emotions. Plumb the depths of your heartbreak. Come to grips with how unfair life is and how cruelly you've been treated. And whatever you do, don't mix God-talk into your pain. That only leads to deception."

There's certainly no denial in that approach. There's no glossing or "spiritualizing." But there's also no hope, no answer to people's despair. As they abandon their faith in God, they plummet into the abyss of personal agony and eventually become sickened with self-pity and hopelessness.

They take their eyes off Christ, stop reading the Bible, stop praying, and stop listening to the encouragement of Christian friends. They isolate themselves from all avenues of divine intervention and slide into utter despair. And in the end, they quietly whisper, "Where's God in all this? Does He have *no* role to play in my attempt to cope? Must I face the rogue winds of life all alone?"

Philippians 4:4 obviously decries that approach. But I believe the spirit of the verse also decries the first approach. I want to show in this chapter that the kind of rejoicing Paul spoke of required no overspiritualized denial of emotional authenticity. His "rejoicing" required a rugged, mature faith that authentically acknowledged both the pains of life and the power of God.

PAUL'S PERSPECTIVE

The first chapter of Philippians gives a glimpse into the context from which Paul admonished his readers to rejoice. To begin with, he was in prison. What made that especially distressing was that something terrible was happening outside his locked cell. Hucksters were on the circuit, preaching Christ with impure motives and taking up offerings to fill their own pockets.

It was unthinkable to Paul that people would use the Gospel of Christ to elevate themselves and build personal empires. Besides, it was unfair. Evil men were free to preach, while Paul, who loved the Lord sincerely, was locked in a prison cell.

Certainly Paul had little reason to rejoice. And he *didn't* rejoice— at least not about being in prison or about evil men "using" the message of Christ. But read what he wrote in Philippians 1:18: "But what does it matter? The important thing is that in every way, whether from false motives or true, Christ is preached. And because of this I rejoice." What did he rejoice in? That Christ was being preached.

He didn't gloss over the issue of hucksters. He didn't try to convince the readers of his letter that everything was peachy in Philippi. He said, "There's something rotten going on here. And it distresses me deeply." On the other hand, he didn't dwell on the damage of the hucksters and drown himself and others in seas of despair. He didn't say, "The church in Philippi is doomed. We might as well close up shop and go home."

Paul acknowledged the hucksters, openly lamented their threat, then placed the whole tragedy in the context of God's overall activity in the world. That freed him to rejoice in the one little part of the whole fiasco that was indeed praiseworthy: that even if it was done for wrong motives, at least Christ was being preached. In that, Paul could genuinely rejoice.

Philippians 2:14–18 provides another illustration of Paul's style of rejoicing. In this passage Paul challenges his readers to "become blameless and pure, children of God without fault in a crooked and depraved generation." Why did he want them to do this? So that "I may boast on the day of Christ that I did not run or labor for nothing." Paul wanted them to remain steadfast in their faith so he could rejoice in two things. First, that his efforts to establish and nurture that little group of believers had lead to genuinely transformed lives. And second, that someday he would receive a reward from the Lord for his faithful service.

He continued with these words: "Even if I am being poured out like a drink offering on the sacrifice and service coming from your faith, I am glad and rejoice." In the midst of beatings, imprisonment, and impending death there was something Paul could sincerely rejoice in.

Paul didn't deny the reality of the situation. He openly acknowledged that he was sitting on death row, "being poured out like a drink offering." But he didn't drown in self-pity because of that. He found something in that ugly situation worth rejoicing about: that lives had been changed and someday he would be rewarded for his part in that process. That's what he chose to focus on.

Paul gives a final, simple challenge to his Philippian readers to "Rejoice in the Lord always. I will say it again: Rejoice!" (Phil. 4:4). In other words, "Do what I did. Whatever situation you're in, find something praiseworthy. Don't deny the problems. Don't ignore the hurt. But find some little part of the situation that's praiseworthy, and in that you can 'rejoice in the Lord always.'"

A CONTEMPORARY EXAMPLE

Benjamin Weir, a Presbyterian minister, wrote about his struggle to maintain sanity and emotional equilibrium during his sixteen months as a hostage in Beirut.

> As the first days of June passed, I began to realize there were two different ways to regard the passage of time. One was to regret each day as freedom lost, twenty-four hours of my life spent without profit. This was true. I did yearn to be active. I also longed to be close to Carol and in touch with my family. However, to concentrate on this kind of regret would only be frustrating and depressing.
>
> Perhaps practical faith and hope and the will to survive required a different point of view. So I chose to add up the days with a sense of achievement, insofar as possible. At day's end I would say to myself, *Well, you made it through another day. Now you must have strength for the next one.*
>
> As the light dimmed, I would sing to myself, "Now the day is over. / Night is drawing nigh. / Shadows of the evening steal across the sky." And I would thank God for providing me with resources and stamina beyond my expectation.
>
> In the morning, I would thank God for another day of living, refreshing sleep, sound body, and assurance of his sustaining presence. After my first exercise period, I would do my Bible "reading," recalling passages that came to memory. I reviewed various psalms and fragments of them. I would choose each day a figure from the Old Testament—Abraham, Isaac, Jacob, Joseph, Gideon, Samuel, Saul—and tell myself his story of faith.
>
> I tried to reconstruct the account of Jesus from his birth to his resurrection. I detailed the travels of Paul, adding with mental pictures those places in the story that I had visited. I was astounded at Paul's persistence in the face of obstacles and dangers; I returned again and again to Romans 8:28: "In everything God works for good with those who love him, who are called according to his purpose." This assurance was the foundation for my grip on sanity and hope.[1]

Benjamin Weir discovered the formula Paul used. Lament loss. Grieve over death and separation. Get angry about tyranny and inequity. Be saddened by the disappointments of life. But put those heartbreaks into the overall context of the ongoing activity of God in the world, your life, and in eternity. Then focus on the praiseworthy portion of the situation so you can rejoice authentically.

PERPLEXED BUT NOT DESPAIRING

Paul applied this principle repeatedly. He wrote to the Corinthian church, "We are hard pressed on every side, but not crushed; perplexed, but not in despair; persecuted, but not abandoned; struck down, but not destroyed. We always carry around in our body the death of Jesus, so that the life of Jesus may also be revealed in our body" (2 Cor. 4:8–10).

Paul again acknowledged the dreadful reality of living in a sin-stained, evil-tarnished world. He said we're hard-pressed, perplexed, persecuted, and struck down. But true to form, he looked beyond the pain to something he could rejoice in. There may be pain, he said, but it will neither crush us nor throw us into despair; we'll be neither abandoned nor destroyed.

Why? Because "we know that the one who raised the Lord Jesus from the dead will also raise us with Jesus and present us with you in his presence" (2 Cor. 4:14). In the fiercest storms and the darkest nights, when there's not one iota of temporal comfort to cling to, Paul rejoices in the eternal reality of heaven. The day is coming when the same power that raised Jesus from the dead is going to raise him to life eternal!

WHAT ABOUT US?

That's a nice little Bible study. But what do Paul's words mean to us today? What do we do if we're neck-deep in marital troubles, or child-rearing frustrations, or financial, physical, or vocational difficulties? What do we do if we're carrying around unfinished business that bogs us down in an emotional quagmire? How do we get from here to authentic rejoicing?

First, refuse to deny the pain, the frustration, or the heartache. Denying our difficulties or pretending they don't debilitate us in various ways is deceitful. Thoughtlessly chanting "Praise the Lord Anyway" is not being real. So let's go beyond that. Let's drop the hypocrisy and be honest with ourselves.

Sure, it's hard to give up our Norman Rockwell picture of life, but that's not reality. Reality is that our parents were imperfect and behaved in ways that brought us pain. Reality is that miscarriages cause grief. Reality is that wayward teenagers can rip a parent's heart out. Reality is that losing a job can create feelings of fear and anxiety. Reality is that sexual abuse causes devastation. Reality is that there is heartache in this world, and sometimes you and I are caught in the middle of it.

When that's true, we need to acknowledge our gut-level responses. We need to admit to ourselves that we're afraid, lonely, disappointed, or angry.

The second step is to honestly tell God how we feel. He can handle our authentic cries of pain and disappointment. He can even help us work through them.

That was a hard thing for me to grasp, because my religious background placed tremendous emphasis on God's transcendence. I heard over and over again that God was sovereign and holy. That's true, but it was so overemphasized that it led to a deterministic theology. It said, in effect, "God decreed it, so don't ask questions. Just be quiet and go along with the program."

Then I started reading the Bible on my own and was totally tripped up by the Psalms. Repeatedly David expressed his heartfelt confusion: "God, I don't understand this. How can You treat me this way? How can You allow this? Why do the righteous suffer while the wicked prosper? Help me understand this!" David, "a man after God's own heart," certainly had no God-decreed-it-so-don't-ask-questions mindset. (See Ps. 73.)

What I've learned is that often these authentic outpourings of frustration, or even anger, are necessary steps on the path to wholeness. The cathartic process of pouring our hearts out to the Lord, of emptying ourselves of pent-up emotions and unanswered questions, opens the way for insight and understanding.

The same thing happens to us that so often happened to the psalmist. After the outburst comes the renewed perspective. The lights go on. We realize anew that in spite of the heartache or the unanswered questions, God is still God. There is still hope. We still matter to Him. The Holy Spirit still lives in us. The Bible is still true. The church is still intact. Heaven still awaits. And in that we can rejoice.

What does this mean for the sexually abused woman described at the beginning of this chapter? It means she can pound her clenched fists on the table and scream, "God, why didn't you stop my father? Why'd you let him hurt me again and again? If you're a loving God, how could you stand to watch it happen? Are you so powerless you couldn't do anything about it? Or are you simply not there at all?"

For a woman as violently abused as that woman was, those are inevitable questions. Emotional authenticity demands that she ask them. And it demands that she ask them over and over again, for however long it takes her to reestablish genuine faith in God. If she doesn't, she'll become an inauthentic Christian who goes through the motions of believing in God, but has no inner confidence in His power or His love.

If you were to look in my journal, you would find my frustrations, fears, and questions spilled all over its pages. But you'd also find a written record of the assurances and promises God has given me in return. The day after my father's death, I poured out my fear to the Lord. I knew I was facing the greatest ministry challenges I had ever faced. How could I face them without the person who had been my greatest cheerleader, the one who had always made me believe I could "handle anything"? God answered my heart's cry by assuring me that if I would abide in Him, He would become my encourager. He would make me strong.

The third step is to discuss our pain, our disappointment, or our heartache with someone else. I can't tell you how many times people have approached me at church, with tears in their eyes, to tell me something they've "never told anyone before." Haltingly, they report a childhood incident that still haunts them and makes them feel fearful and insecure. Or they tell how disappointed they are with their marriage and how they've been trying to deny the disappointment and pretend everything is okay.

They finish their story and say, "I don't know why, but I feel better now. Maybe now I can talk to my husband [or my wife, or my friend, or my small-group leader] about this."

There is healing power in sharing our inner hurts with someone else. There's a release, a catharsis, that makes the burden seem lighter. Sometimes just having someone affirm the legitimacy of our pain eases it a little. There's also the obvious benefit of receiving guidance from those with whom we share. Overwhelming issues suddenly become manageable when a friend offers an insight or suggests a course of action we hadn't thought of.

At times, however, our friends can't help enough. That brings me to my last point. Sometimes our unfinished business is so weighty and emotionally debilitating that we need to seek professional help.

That was true for each of the people described in the first pages of this chapter. The victim of sexual abuse had experienced such extreme violation that it took years of intense therapy to heal the damage. The other woman had created such a convincing image of toughness and invincibility that only a trained counselor could trace her uncontrollable tears to years of buried grief. And only a person trained to deal with compulsive behaviors could uncover the unmet needs driving the successful businessman to overeat himself into obesity.

God doesn't ask us to spiritualize these and other painful realities away. Certainly the healing process requires divine intervention and spiritual growth. And often loving family and friends can provide the human support and wisdom we need. But there are times when competent Christian counselors can provide the necessary blend of spiritual and psychological perspectives. They can help us uncover and understand significant events in our past. And they can help us resolve tensions and initiate more positive relationships with significant people in our lives.

A PERSONAL CRUSADE

I am particularly concerned about the issue of sexual abuse because it is so much more common, and so much more destructive, than most people realize. Several years ago I gave a message on sexual abuse and was deluged with letters from women who said, "That was me you were talking about. Please help me!"

The ramifications of childhood sexual abuse are too numerous to examine fully here, but I want to list six of the most significant ones.

1. *Hatred toward the offender.* This often escalates after the abuse ceases, and the victim reflects not only on what was, but on what should have been. Over time, it commonly expands into a more general kind of rage directed at society and God.

2. *Mistrust of other people, particularly male authority figures.* These women learned at a young age that when they submitted to men, they were abused. This often causes them to be generally rebellious.

3. *Guilt.* Even though they were the victims, they often feel cheap and dirty.

4. *Poor self-esteem.* They feel stained. When they look at others they think, "If you knew the truth about me. . . ."

5. *Diminished desire for sexual activity in marriage.* For years, every touch was like a branding iron. How can it suddenly be experienced as pleasurable?

6. *Dependence on drugs and alcohol.* How do you deal with a twenty-four-hour-a-day nightmare? You do whatever you can do to escape from the memories.

It's obvious why counseling is required to help women work through ramifications like these, and these are only a few of the possible negative results. If you know anyone who has experienced sexual abuse, please encourage them to talk with an experienced Christian counselor.

BACK TO PAUL

Paul's call to a life of rejoicing doesn't mean a life of cheap slogans and bumper-sticker solutions. Authentic Christianity gives us room to honestly deal with the heartache in our lives by acknowledging it, pouring it out to the Lord, and sharing it with friends and counselors.

But the last step still remains—to find in every situation, no matter how distressing, that little bit of reality that's worthy of praise. In that the true child of God can authentically rejoice.

I can't end this chapter without urging those of you with buried pain to step out in faith. Begin to process the pain in the ways I described in this chapter. Jesus said, "So if the Son sets you free, you will be free indeed" (John 8:36). God wants you to be free from the inner turmoil that haunts you.

Why not decide right now to take steps toward emotional healing? It's possible your journey will take you through the valley—that you'll dredge up pain you think is too great to bear. But as hard as it is, it's a price worth paying. It's the only path to the freedom of emotional authenticity.

NOTES

1. Benjamin M. Weir, with Dennis Benson, "Tough Faith," *Leadership Journal* 10, no. 1 (Winter 1989), 58–59.

9

Energized for Effective Service

Once the mask of artificial emotions comes off, a Christian is ready to truly serve others, in an authentic way. But service can still occur in the wrong ways, for the wrong reasons.

It's August. Throughout the country, the late summer ritual begins. And it's not a pretty sight.

Pastor Bob has just received his annual flood of resignation notes. Sunday school teachers, ushers, Bible study leaders, youth leaders, and assorted other "servers" have called it quits. He's not surprised. It happens every year. Some people offer lengthy explanations. Others say simply, "I've done my part."

Now Pastor Bob knows that the ministries of the church can't continue unless someone fills all these empty positions. So, with unprecedented determination, be begins psyching up for the annual "August Recruitment Campaign."

Pastor Bob isn't the first to fight this battle. His predecessor fought it, too. In fact, it's become somewhat of a tradition—one that even his most tradition-bound congregants would like to do without. So, while Pastor Bob is psyching himself up, his two hundred members are doing the same. They know they'll have to be tough to resist this year's recruitment campaign. It's going to be war!

A man named Jim says to himself, "He's not going to get me this year. So help me, I don't care what he preaches on, or how often he threatens God's judgment. I'm not going to cave in—even if he starts to cry! Three years ago he cried and I ended up as a center aisle usher—and I don't even like people. This year I'll resist to the end."

Pastor Bob does know how much resistance has surfaced in his congregation. So this year he's bringing out the heavy artillery. He's planning a four-sided series called "Serve or Burn." Every week he'll use a dramatic illustration from *Foxe's Book of Martyrs.* There's nothing like true-to-life stories of people who gave up their lives for serving Christ.

He's already decided to wear a lapel microphone. Then he can walk the length of the stage, raise his voice, perspire a little bit, and wave his Bible in the air.

On the fourth week, he'll bring out his secret weapon. Seven-year-old Suzi Miller. He'll cradle the little darling on his lap and ask her what it will be like to spend a whole year in second grade Sunday school with no teacher.

He hopes against hope that she'll cry. If she does, he'll win the war hands down. Sure as shootin' he'll win the war.

So the stage is set. It's going to be an interesting August.

DISASTER

Let's just suppose Paster Bob's strategy works. The "Serve or Burn" series goes better than he expected. Little Suzi cries on cue. People feel worn down and guilty. And by September 1, the empty positions are filled for another year.

But what happens over the course of that year? Is there "joy in serving Jesus"?

Of course not. When people serve because they "lost the war," they end up serving inauthentically, for the wrong reasons. They do it out of guilt. Or to get the pastor off their back. Or maybe just to look good to other people.

They also frequently end up serving in the wrong areas. If the pastor's only concern is filling open slots, he won't care who ends up doing what. If a sensitive person visits in August, he'll probably end up teaching little Suzi's Sunday school class.

"What? You're a brand-new Christian? That's okay. Sometimes the teacher learns more than the students."

But what happens to a Sunday school class taught by an ill-equipped teacher? The kids are usually out of control; they don't learn much. Morale in the youth department wanes because no one wants to go to class. The teacher feels frustrated and unfulfilled, so he resigns the first chance he gets . . . as does the introverted center aisle usher, the hospitality chairman who can't cook, the offering counter who hates detail work, and the song leader who can't carry a tune.

Next year there are more resignations than ever, and the recruitment war reaches new heights of viciousness.

What a pitiful situation. Isn't there a better way?

THANK YOU, GOD

Yes. It's called authentic service.

It has two essential characteristics. First, it flows naturally out of worship. Second, it takes into account the unique giftedness of the server.

If you've ever served for any motivation besides worship, you were an inauthentic server. Service that pleases God is a heartfelt response for all that He has done. Authentic servers realize that they are sinners deserving eternal condemnation. They can do nothing to earn God's favor. Only Jesus' death on their behalf buys their entrance into heaven.

They know too what it means to be adopted into the family of God and to be able to address the almighty God of the universe as Father. They know what it means to be indwelt by the Holy Spirit and have access to divine power. They have the assurance of a future in heaven, where all grief and hardship will be wiped away.

People who grasp the reality of all they have in Christ can't help but respond with worship and gratitude. They find themselves laying awake at night thinking up ways to show their gratitude for God's amazing grace. Like the psalmist they ask, "How can I repay the Lord for all his goodness to me?" (Ps. 116:12).

Authentic service is a genuine attempt to say "Thank You" to God. If you read through the last few paragraphs without feeling motivated to do that, read them again. If that doesn't help, go for a long walk and humble yourself before God. Confess pride about self and about accomplishments. Ask His forgiveness for being so calloused to His miracles. Ask Him to open your eyes to the spiritual blessings He's poured into your life.

Paul said, "I consider my life worth nothing to me, if only I may finish the race and complete the task the Lord Jesus has given me—the task of testifying to the gospel of God's grace" (Acts 20:24). Paul's greatest desire was to pursue the task—the service—to which God had called him. This was his response of thanksgiving and worship, a response more dear than life itself.

Paul said that if we want to show our thanks to God, we need to make our lives a living sacrifice of praise (Rom. 12:1). We need to crawl up on the altar and offer our entire lives as worship to the Lord.

How do we do that?

Praise. First, we can worship God with our thoughts and words of praise. We do that when we write our prayers of adoration each morning and sing worship songs or listen to them in our car. We do it every time we look at the miracles of nature and give God glory for His handiwork. We can do it continually in the classroom, at the job site, while we're running, in the office, or in traffic. God delights in our words of praise and rewards us with His presence.

Giving. Offering God our material resources is another form of worship. God warns against offering "blemished lambs"—offerings that cost us nothing—but He's pleased when we offer generous gifts with joyful hearts. He rewards the giver with the promise of His help.

Evangelism. We also worship God when we share our faith with others. What greater joy can we give God than to help someone begin a relationship with Him?

Service. Finally, we worship God through our service. The authentic server views each opportunity to lead or serve as an opportunity to worship God. And God accepts the offering with its pleasing aroma of praise.

FIRST THINGS FIRST

The apostle Paul was quick to tell those who were purely motivated to serve that they shouldn't just run out and sign up for the first job that comes along. They shouldn't just "fill a position" for a year, then bail out. They shouldn't let Pastor Bob threaten them into service that seems more like a prison term than an act of worship.

If we want to worship God by serving, we need to do it right. We need first to take time to determine our spiritual gifts. Those are the unique abilities God places in each of us at the moment of salvation that enable us to build up and encourage other believers in the church.

Four primary biblical texts teach about spiritual gifts: 1 Corinthians 12–14; Romans 12:1–8; Ephesians 4:1–16; 1 Peter 4:8–11. For simplification, the gifts mentioned in these passages can be listed in four categories.

Speaking Gifts

Prophecy	Teaching

People Intensive Gifts

Counseling	Hospitality
Creative Communications	Leadership
Encouragement	Mercy
Evangelism	Shepherding

Service Gifts

Administration	Giving
Craftsmanship	Helps

Support Gifts

Apostleship	Knowledge
Discernment	Miracles
Faith	Tongues
Healing	Wisdom
Interpretation	

There's not room in this chapter to fully explain each of these gifts. But even a simple listing reveals the variety of abilities God places in His children.

We need to take these abilities seriously. Paul said, "Now about spiritual gifts, brothers, I do not want you to be ignorant" (1 Cor. 12:1). To Timothy he said, "Do not neglect your gift. . . . Be diligent in these matters; give yourself wholly to them. . . . Persevere in them (1 Tim. 4:14–16).

God will hold us accountable for the use of our spiritual gifts. "Each one should use whatever gift he has received to serve others, faithfully administering God's grace in its various forms" (1 Pet. 4:10). An administrator is one who manages another's affairs. When God tells us to administer our spiritual gifts, He's telling us to use them faithfully and diligently, as resources He's entrusted to our care.

Do you know your spiritual gifts? Are you using them as acts of worship to God?

If not, now is the time to begin. If you need further information, there are books and tapes on spiritual gifts. Some books I would suggest are *Team Ministry* by Larry Gilbert and *Networking* by Bruce Bugbee. If you're still not convinced that it's worth your time, jump to the end of this chapter and read about the results of authentic service. Christians who don't know their spiritual gifts and aren't serving in the right place are missing out on some of the greatest blessings of the Christian life.

PASSION

Another important element to consider in determining where and how to serve the Lord, is your passion. Let me explain.

James Dobson, Luis Palau, John Perkins, and R. C. Sproul are all respected leaders in the Christian community. They each have ministries with national or international impact. Yet if you compare their respective ministries, you'll find that they are each directed to different audiences. Why? Because they have different passions.

James Dobson, founder of Focus on the Family ministries and radio program, has a passion for the family. I've spent enough time with Jim to know that if you get him talking about the family, you better have plenty of time to listen. There's nothing he'd rather talk about than the condition, needs, value, and future of the family. It's his passion, and he applies all his gifts to building it up. His books, films, radio program, and entire ministry are devoted to it.

Luis Palau, international evangelist, has a passion for the lost. What turns his crank are stadiums full of people who need the Lord. He says, "Give me the gospel and some good music, and we'll do damage in enemy territory. We'll lead people to the Lord." He goes from crusade to crusade, country to country, reaching the lost.

John Perkins, founder of Voice of Calvary Ministries, has a passion for minorities and the inner-city needy. So he devotes all his gifts to setting up programs to help them find dignity and self-esteem through meaningful employment opportunities.

R. C. Sproul, well-respected theologian and author, has a passion to study and teach the very deepest truths of the Christian faith. He likes to get small groups of seminarians together to discuss cosmological arguments for the existence of God. After that, he moves on to the heavy stuff! More than once, while listening to R.C., I've felt like the train left and I was still standing at the station. But that's his passion.

These are multigifted men who could serve in many other ways. Why don't they? Because they have a specific passion that calls them to a specific ministry, and they love what they do. If they tried to swap ministries, they couldn't do it authentically—not because they don't have the gifts, but because they don't have the right passion.

Do you know your passion? If not, ask yourself these questions:

1. What local, global, political, social, or church issues stir you emotionally?
2. What group of people do you feel most attracted to?
3. What area of need is of ultimate importance to you?
4. If you knew you could not fail, what would you do with your life?
5. What area of your church's ministry would you most like to influence?

Answering these questions may help you detect a passion for unwed mothers, the poor, unbelievers, youth, discipleship, the sick, or business executives. You may notice that this passion is related to your heritage or past experiences. For example, growing up in a broken home may give you a passion to minister to children of single parents. Or growing up with a live-in grandparent may spark a passion to minister to the elderly.

Once you determine your passion, think of ways to use your gifts in conjunction with your passion. If your passion is for junior high students and your gift is helping, you might offer your services to the youth director at your church—to set up equipment, chauffeur students, or send out mailings.

If your passion is for young moms and your gift is teaching, you might start a Bible study for them. If your gift is helping, you could volunteer to baby-sit for their children during the Bible study. If your gift is mercy, you could prepare meals for them when they're sick.

There are, you see, many different ways to serve. Paul says, "There are different kinds of gifts, but the same Spirit. There are different kinds of service, but the same Lord. There are different kinds of working, but the same God works all of them in all men" (1 Cor. 12:4–7).

TEMPERAMENT

Another factor that determines how and where we serve is our temperament.

One reason James Dobson is so good at what he does is that by nature he's a warm, relational person who puts others at ease. His radio guests feel like they're talking to an old friend, so they open up and talk naturally. Even Jim's voice coming over the radio sounds down-to-earth and friendly. It makes you want to get comfortable in an easy chair and tune in to his broadcast.

One of the secrets of Luis Palau's success is that his personality shines in a stadium. The minute he walks out on the platform, his exuberance grabs your attention. It doesn't matter what he says; you have to listen.

R.C. is great in front of a crowd, but what he really loves is solitude. And it's a good thing. The key to amassing the amount of knowledge he has is long, solitary hours of reading and studying. R.C.'s tapes on "The Holiness of God" impacted me more than any tapes I've ever listened to. I thank God that his personality allowed him to spend hours alone, putting that series together.

John Perkins is a quiet, thoughtful man. He doesn't walk into a room and bowl you over with his presence. He just slips in and fits in with the group. Certainly that's one of the keys to his success in working with the downtrodden. His temperament is gentle enough to be nonthreatening and encouraging.

What are the characteristics of your temperament? If you need to, look back at the chapter on marriage. Are you an introvert? Then don't choose an area of service that's too people-intensive. If you're an extrovert, don't end up in a ministry that demands lots of solitude.

If you're a feeler, avoid positions that require heavy doses of confrontation or black-and-white decision making. Thinkers may be more comfortable in forms of service that deal with strategies and decisions rather than with people.

THE CHURCH ALIVE

One of the results of authentic service is that it pleases God. It delights the heart of the One who redeemed us and made us for meaningful service.

But authentic service also benefits the church. People who serve for the right reason and in the right place are enthusiastic and effective. Their teaching has impact. Their hospitality is warm. Their counsel is wise. Their leadership is strong. Their administration is efficient. Their evangelism is fruitful. Their mercy is heartfelt.

Speaking of mercy, it's no secret to those who know me that I don't have that gift. Not long ago at an elders' meeting I prayed with a dear woman from our church who is slowly dying of diabetes. As much as I loved this woman and wanted to minister to her, I was painfully aware of my awkwardness. I just don't function well in situations like that.

After I left this woman, another elder approached her. Without hesitation he wrapped his arms around her, kissed her on the cheek, and said, "Oh, Jane, I'm so glad you're here tonight." While he held her hand she wept. Because he was so natural and tender, she could really feel his love and concern.

I thought, "Lord, thank You for giving him that beautiful gift of mercy. Thank You for prompting him to use it here tonight."

The whole body benefits when things like that happen. People's needs are met. Morale is high. Excellence becomes the mark of existing ministries, because people are doing what they do best. New ministries start as an expression of the varied gifts, passions, and temperaments of the members. Church becomes an exciting place.

IT FEELS SO GOOD TO SERVE

The church isn't the only benefactor. Servers themselves benefit by experiencing fulfillment that they've never known before.

Recently a man said to me, "I love leading small groups. I started with a group of brand new Christians. After two years they left the group mature and ready to make a mark for Jesus Christ. You tell me what beats that."

I asked him if he was going to lead another group. "Of course. I can't wait to get started."

Other people say, "I love working with junior high students. They're so needy and hungry for love. I get such a thrill when they finally trust me enough to open up. It's great!"

One of the men on our board of directors, a dentist, called me this morning and said, "I have two 'numbing up' in the chair, so I just have a minute, but I have to run something by you." There he was, in the middle of his workday, snatching a minute for church business. I could hear the excitement in his voice. He has the gift of administration, and he loves to use it.

Other people say, "I love my Sunday school kids. I can't wait till Sunday morning rolls along." We have teachers who have been teaching for ten years. Why don't they resign every July? Because they're so fulfilled in what they do. It's worship. It's in keeping with their gifts, passions, and temperaments. And on top of that, they receive affirmation.

When you're serving for the right reason in the right place, people notice and appreciate your effort.

"You're making a real contribution. We need what you're offering. We couldn't continue this ministry without you. Thank you for sharing yourself and your talents with us."

It's great to hear words like that. God wants us to serve in such a way that we can receive that kind of response.

ESPRIT DE CORPS

When a group of people serve together, a common spirit of enthusiasm is generated. Let me illustrate.

At our church, we have a traffic safety team that directs traffic every time we have services. In the Midwest, that means they stand outside in everything from scorching heat waves to sub-zero snowstorms.

Last Easter, which was unusually cold and rainy, our traffic safety team had to direct traffic Thursday and Friday nights, and on Sunday from 4:00 A.M. to 2:00 P.M. I expected that by Sunday afternoon we'd have to scrape them off the pavement.

Instead I found them having a tailgate party! As I walked to my car they offered me coffee and cookies.

"Wasn't it a great day?!" they said. "There were so many people here, we had to park 'em on the ball diamonds. And they all heard the message of the Resurrection. What a day!"

Those people are using their gifts of "helps" in the right place for the right reason. And they're enjoying yet another of the blessed by-products of authentic service. Fellowship. There's nothing like the camaraderie that develops in the trenches of service.

Over the years I've heard many people complain about the lack of genuine fellowship in the church. But I've never heard that complaint made by someone who's involved in authentic service. Service draws people together in the pursuit of common goals. That inevitably opens the door to significant relationships.

WHAT A FIND

When you're enjoying the fulfillment and fellowship that inevitably accompanies authentic service, ministry is a joy. Instead of exhausting you, it energizes you. Instead of burnout you experience blessing. You say, "It's a privilege. I want to do this for the rest of my life!"

When service makes you feel that way, you never even think of resigning. In fact, a team of wild horses couldn't pull you away from your post of service.

After I gave a message on this subject at a pastor's conference, a pastor wrote me a brief note. "You're the first person I've ever told this to. I've been a senior pastor for twenty-three years and I've never enjoyed it, because I've been so frustrated with preaching. You helped me understand that I don't have preaching gifts, I don't have a passion to reach people in mass groups, and my temperament is too laid-back for up-front effectiveness. What I really love to do is visit people in the hospital and comfort the grieving."

This man is now serving in a church as minister of visitation and counseling, and he's happy, effective, and fulfilled. He loves his ministry because it's in perfect sync with who God made him to be.

Serving is a vital part of the authentic Christian life. But to be right it has to flow out of worship, and it has to fit who God made you to be. A person can love Jesus Christ with all his heart, soul, mind, and strength, but if his service doesn't fit that criteria, it will never flourish and it will only lead to frustration.

If that has happened to you, you've probably sworn off service for the rest of your life.

Can I get you to reconsider? Why not try it the right way this time? Determine your spiritual gifts, your passion, and your temperament preferences. Then place yourself at God's disposal and see what happens. He knows you're an utterly unique individual, and has a special task designed just for you.

10

Unstereotyping Evangelism

Those who are anxious to gain new strategies and skills in evangelism rarely need motivation to get into a chapter like this. But some of you are thinking of skipping this chapter. You believe that making evangelism authentic is about as easy as making a hospital stay fun.

Just the thought of evangelism strikes terror in you! It awakens unwanted feelings of fear, pressure, and guilt. You grew up under teachers who overemphasized personal evangelism and established unrealistic expectations.

Years ago I attended a conference where the speaker informed us that if we really loved Jesus Christ, we'd share Christ with three people before we went to bed that night. Nearly everyone in the auditorium signaled their acceptance of his challenge by jumping to their feet. I noted it was nearly 10:00 P.M. and refused to respond to his ridiculous, manipulative appeal. I stayed in my seat—and felt humiliated and guilty.

Others of you are introverts who have been repeatedly intimidated by extroverted teachers who can't understand why witnessing to strangers on street corners is such a "stretch" for you. "Don't you *care* about people?" they ask. You hate to admit that every attempt you've made to tell strangers about Christ has been an outright disaster.

I have no intention of loading another burden on your back. Authentic evangelism is never motivated by guilt. It's part of an overall transformed mindset, and it's built around the belief that every individual has a unique, God-ordained evangelistic style and enjoys fruitfulness and freedom in witnessing only when using that style. Authentic evangelism fills the evangelist with anticipation and confidence, not terror.

In this chapter I would like to discuss the three facets of authentic evangelism: motivation, mindset, and style.

MOTIVATION

We've Got It All!

The first motivation for personal evangelism is what I call the "stockpile factor."

Second Kings 6–7 records the story of the siege of Samaria by the king of Aram. Because of the siege and a great famine in the land, the city experienced a food shortage so severe it drove the people to cannibalism. To survive, mothers literally ate their children. Doomed to die with the rest of the city, four outcast lepers decided on a desperate plan: to enter the camp of the Arameans and surrender. They said, "If they spare us, we live; if they kill us, then we die" (2 Kings 7:4).

To their amazement, the lepers found the camp deserted. God had caused the Aramean army "to hear the sound of chariots and horses and a great army" (2 Kings 7:6). The Arameans concluded that the king of Israel had hired the Hittites and Egyptians to attack them. Terrified, they fled for their lives, leaving everything in the camp behind.

The lepers were beside themselves! They rushed from tent to tent, feasting and looting. They filled their arms with treasures of silver and gold, and gathered mounds of clothes that would last them for years. Hurriedly they hid their plunder, then ran back for more.

But their frantic hoarding was cut short. "We're not doing right. This is a day of good news and we are keeping it to ourselves. Let's go at once and report this to the royal palace" (2 Kings 7:9). They did, and the entire city enjoyed the abundance of the Aramean camp.

Why did the lepers share the secret of the abandoned camp? Because of the "stockpile factor." They were overwhelmed by their unexpected good fortune. They were awed by the provision that had been divinely supplied for them. They knew it was a crime to keep the incredible bounty of God's blessing all to themselves.

With tears in his eyes, a young man told me of the recent work of God in his life. "He did something so fantastic for me, I'm about ready to explode!" For fifteen minutes he told of his recent conversion, of the transformation taking place in his marriage, and of divine guidance regarding a housing crisis. "What a wonderful God we have," he said. "I just can't keep quiet about Him!"

When true believers are awed by the greatness of God and by the privilege of becoming His children, then they become sincerely motivated, effective evangelists. They find themselves saying naturally with the psalmist, "Taste and see that the Lord is good" (Ps. 34:8). With little strategy or effort they find fitting opportunities to share with seekers their confidence in God's goodness, wisdom, and power. "I don't know about you," they say, "but I've found God to be so wonderful, I would be a fool not to serve Him."

When I see seekers who matter to God poking around the garbage heaps for meaning in life; when I see them dashing from bar to bar, lover to lover, toy to toy, fun-fix to fun-fix; when I see them repeatedly turn down dead-end streets—I fill with pity and want to shout, "Stop your endless searching! Stop picking at refuse piles! Experience God's love. The stockpile of His blessing is waiting to spill over into your life."

Why aren't more believers motivated by the "stockpile factor"? Because Satan does everything in his power to convince spiritual princes that they're paupers. If he can make us lose sight of our wealth, he can render us ineffective as evangelists.

That is why each of us needs a daily refresher course on the scope of our blessings. One way that happens for me is by keeping a journal and writing out my thanks to God. (See Chapter 2.)

Every time I go over my stockpile, I become filled with a sense of spiritual wonder. I think, "Why would anyone *not* want to be in a relationship with our wonderful God?" That makes for confident evangelism.

Agent 00

The second motivation for personal evangelism is the honor of being an agent of God. Jesus told His followers, "But you will receive power when the Holy Spirit comes on you; and you will be my witnesses in Jerusalem, and in all Judea and Samaria, and to the ends of the earth" (Acts 1:8).

As remarkable as it seems, God chooses ordinary people to be His spokespersons on planet Earth. To every believer like you or me He says, "You are My special agent. You are the person I need to reach a certain group of humans in a corner of My world. They need your personality, your abilities, your perspective on life, your age factor, your sense of humor, and your message. They need *you*, filled with the Holy Spirit, and commissioned as My agent of peace and reconciliation." That commission motivates me!

What's the key to being effectively used by God? A humble, submissive heart that's tuned in to the Holy Spirit. Jesus said, *"You will receive power when the Holy Spirit has come upon you."* When I'm preoccupied with my own agenda, I stumble upon few opportunities to be God's spokesperson. But if I quiet myself in the morning, give my day to the Lord, and ask Him to work through me, I often find opportunities and sense God's power at work.

Eternity

The third motivation for becoming an effective evangelist is one I'd rather not mention: the reality of hell.

I hate thinking about it, teaching about it, and writing about it. But the plain truth is that hell *is* real and real people go there for eternity.

The reality of hell was a major theme in Jesus' evangelistic ministry. Jesus grieved over the rich young ruler because He knew he was walking the road to hell. He wept over the people of Jerusalem because He saw them as sheep without a Shepherd; it was only a matter of time before they'd wander off the cliffs of eternity and into the abyss of hell. He narrated incidents like Lazarus and the rich man (Luke 16:19–31), which plainly told of the agony, and the desperation, of those forever separated from God.

Jesus confronted the Pharisees, the scribes, the tax-gatherers, the politicians, the rich, the poor—anybody and everybody—with the hard truth: Unless they repented and put their faith in Him, they would die in their sin and face eternal condemnation.

Why did Jesus teach from early morning until late at night? Why did He square off against the critics and endure the ridicule? Because it broke His heart to see people headed for hell.

I believe in hell. I believe in it rationally; I believe in it emotionally. I'm not neurotic about it, but I have to admit that it impacts me every day. It bothers me. It jars me out of complacency. It sparks my energies.

Sometimes people ask why the elders of our church place so much emphasis on reaching the nonchurched. Why do we pour so much time, energy, and money into programs, ideas, and additional staff directed toward outreach? The answer is that when you truly believe in hell you develop a "whatever it takes" mentality. You realize that the stakes are sky-high. You're not just playing church; eternal life and death hang in the balance.

The Angels Rejoice

The final motivation for evangelism is the reward of leading someone to Christ.

"You know, I was lost until God brought His message to me through you. Thanks for reaching out to me, answering my questions, and putting up with my rebellion. Thanks for loving me when I wasn't very lovable. Thanks for living a life that matched your message. Thanks for leading me to the God of Grace!"

You only have to hear that one time to become a motivated ambassador.

Scripture tells us that heaven throws a party for every seeker who submits to Christ (Luke 15:3–7). What a thrill to be a part of the cosmic celebration.

MINDSET

Preoccupied with People

"Come, follow me," Jesus said, "and I will make you fishers of men" (Matt. 4:19). With those words, Jesus challenged Peter and Andrew to consider a total world and life-view transformation, a total change in mindset.

It's as if Jesus said, "Peter, Andrew, for years your whole life has revolved around fishing: how to find fish, how to catch fish, how to market fish. Every day you discussed ways to become more effective fishermen. You devoted all your gifts, talents, and abilities to the pursuit of more fish. And that was fine—really it was—until now. But hear Me well, fellows, there's something far more important for you to do now. I want you to find new life in Me; I want you to discover what God is up to in this world; and I want to train you to become fishers of men."

Jesus wasn't saying there was anything wrong with the fishing business—or the construction business, the food business, the travel business, the insurance business, the real estate business. We all need to make a living and take our professions seriously for the glory of God. But He wanted to make the point that there's something far more important than catching fish and bringing them to market: capturing the attention of sinful men and women and bringing them to the cross of Christ. When the two concerns go head-to-head, as they inevitably will, Jesus tells us to major in the people business and minor in the fish business.

Few people are actually asked to leave their nets and abandon their professions. The majority of Jesus' followers are simply asked to develop a new mindset: a mindset that says there's more to life than buying better nets, outfitting bigger boats, and setting new records at the fish market.

Some time ago I talked with a Christian man who owns a number of car dealerships and employs nearly four hundred people. He confessed his dissatisfaction with the impact he'd had on his employees during the previous five years. He felt that his behavior in the marketplace had been no different from that of an atheistic moral humanitarian; there'd been nothing uniquely Christian about his behavior.

He was right. A Christian car dealer ought to do more than sell cars, treat his employees fairly, make a reasonable profit, and be respected in the community. A Christian car dealer ought to get a lump in his throat when he sees faithful employees searching for meaning in the refuse heaps of life. He ought to weep at the thought of them ending up in hell. He ought to lay awake at night thinking of creative ways to reach into their souls and point them to Christ.

The Mindset of Jesus

One of my favorite Scriptures that shows Jesus' emphasis on the ultimate importance of people is Luke 15. According to this passage, the religious leaders were upset because Jesus, who claimed to be the holy Son of God, was hanging around with sinners: He shared meals with cheating tax collectors, arrogant merchants, filthy-mouthed tentmakers, even prostitutes! When Jesus heard the scribes and Pharisees grumbling about His unacceptable associations, He decided to let them know once and for all just how much He loved the very sinners they despised.

He told three moving stories about a lost sheep, a lost coin, and a prodigal son. In each of the stories something of great value is lost, and it matters so much that it warrants either an all-out search or an anguished vigil. When at last the sheep and coin are found, and the son returns home, the respective households burst into songs of rejoicing. Jesus says, "In the same way, I tell you, there is rejoicing in the presence of the angels of God over one sinner who repents" (Luke 15:10).

What's Jesus' message? That lost, wayward, rebellious, cursing people matter to God so much that He wants us to go after them. He wants us to search them out and bring them to Him.

Authentic evangelism flows from a mindset that acknowledges the ultimate value of people—forgotten people, lost people, wandering people, up-and-outers, down-and-outers—all people. The highest value is to love them, serve them, and reach them. Everything else goes up in smoke.

WHAT'S YOUR STYLE?

Picture in your mind the stereotypical evangelist: an animated, extroverted, finger-pointing preacher of hellfire and brimstone. Does that describe you? *Should* it describe you?

Vast numbers of sincere Christians dismiss the subject of evangelism because they can't handle the thought of street corner preaching, door knocking, and Bible thumping. They fear that if they ever get serious about spreading the message of Christ, they'll have to become obnoxious. They'll have to behave in ways that are foreign to them. So they commit themselves to church attendance, Bible reading, prayer, fellowship, giving, and serving, but say a polite "No thanks" to evangelism. They leave that to Extroverted Ed, Dynamic Dave, and Soapbox Sally.

What a tragedy for the church—and for the lost. I believe such thinking is prompted by a satanic scheme to halt the expansion of the kingdom of God. And Satan's strategy has been extremely effective.

How can we counter it? By understanding that there are many styles of effective evangelism. In fact, there are probably as many effective styles as there are evangelists.

Only a tiny fraction of the unbelievers in this world will be reached by the stereotypical evangelist. The unbelieving world is made up of a variety of people: young and old, rich and poor, educated and uneducated, urban and rural, with different races, personalities, values, political systems, and religious backgrounds. Isn't it obvious it would take more than one style of evangelist to reach such a diverse population?

That's where we come in. Somewhere in that multifarious group is a person who needs to hear the message of Christ from someone just like you or me. A person who needs an evangelist of your exact age, career, and level of spiritual understanding, or of my exact personality, background, and interests.

If I make no other point in this chapter, I want to make this one: We don't have to become someone we're not in order to be effective evangelists. We need to be humble; we need to be submitted to the Holy Spirit; we need to be prayerful. Then we simply need to be ourselves and respond naturally to the opportunities God sends our way.

In the remainder of this chapter I want to look at six possible evangelistic styles: confrontational, intellectual, testimonial, relational, invitational, and serving.

"You Crucified the Wrong Man!"—Confrontational

Peter, the transformed fisherman, had a confrontational style of evangelism. In Acts 2 we read Peter's dynamic Pentecost sermon. "Listen carefully to what I say," he began, then proceeded to explain Jesus' fulfillment of the ancient Scriptures and His identity as the Christ. In conclusion, he said, "Therefore let all Israel be assured of this: God has made this Jesus, whom you crucified, both Lord and Christ" (Acts 2:36). In other words, "You crucified the wrong man! You killed the Son of God!"

Pierced to the heart, they asked Peter, "What shall we do?" Peter replied, "Repent and be baptized. . . . Save yourselves from this corrupt generation" (Acts 2:37–40).

Peter exhorted and challenged them. He confidently charged in and hit them with a frontal assault. And it was so effective that three thousand people trusted Christ that day (Acts 2:41). You see, some people will only be reached when they are confronted courageously and straightforwardly with their sin and their need to repent.

And Peter was just the person to do that. He was an "action" person. He was almost always the first person to speak, move, and act. We remember him as the one who walked on water and fell in, but he also was the only one who got out of the boat, the only one willing to take the first step. In the Garden, when Jesus was arrested, Peter grabbed a sword and whacked off a guy's ear. He loved to create action. He liked to stir up controversy. It didn't bother him at all to stand up in front of the masses on Pentecost Day and create a little havoc.

Some people will only come to Christ if they are "knocked over the head with truth" and confronted by someone like Peter. Fortunately, God has equipped certain believers with the combination of personality, gifts, and desires that make it natural for them to confront others.

Have you ever heard Chuck Colson challenge people to receive Christ? He says things like this: "It's high time some of you face the music. You're on the road to hell. You don't have to go there, because Jesus Christ wants to be your Savior. But you're going to end up there unless you repent of your sins, seek forgiveness, and trust Christ."

I doubt that after presenting a challenge like that Chuck goes into a side room and wonders if he was too hard on his listeners. I think he wonders if he hit them hard enough! And thousands of people have come to Christ through his evangelistic efforts.

You may have gathered that I'm a confrontational style evangelist. I love to ask probing questions, spark controversy, create conversational action. Recently a man invited me to address three hundred of his employees at a company luncheon and "lay it on the line." I said, "No problem. That's just what I wanted to do." I don't have to work up courage to do that kind of thing. It is consistent with how God made me.

Often when I relate to Lynne conversations I have with unbelievers, she shudders. "How could you say that? I can't believe it! I could never say something like that!" And she couldn't. God didn't make her for that style of evangelism. But I love it, and as I've submitted myself to the leading of the Holy Spirit, I've sensed that God can use my confrontational style.

Did God make you that way? Then get out there and confront. Offer your personality and passion to the Lord, and ask the Holy Spirit to surround your natural confidence with sensitivity and discernment. Then pray that God will lead you to people who need someone to look them right in the eye and say, "Here's the truth. What are you going to do about it?" They're out there.

Think It Through—Intellectual

Though he could be confrontational like Peter, the apostle Paul often used an intellectual approach to evangelism. In Acts 17 we read that Paul reasoned with the Jews and God-fearing Greeks, "explaining and proving" Christ's resurrection (Acts 17:3). He conversed with the intelligentsia and debated with the philosophers of Athens. In his famous sermon on Mars Hill, he ingeniously used the Athenians' altar to an unknown god as an introduction to his presentation of the true God.

I can imagine Peter in Athens. "What's wrong with you people? Tear down that altar to an unknown god! Repent and worship the true God!" His confrontational approach would never have worked with the intellectuals. They needed a more persuasive, academic approach, like Paul's. We read that in Thessalonica, "Some of the Jews were persuaded and joined Paul and Silas, as did a large number of God-fearing Greeks and not a few prominent women" (Acts 17:4). In Athens, likewise, "A few men became followers of Paul and believed. . . . also a woman named Damaris, and a number of others" (Acts 17:34).

Paul was highly educated, extremely intelligent, and capable of putting together cogent arguments. By nature he loved analyzing, studying, contemplating, and reasoning. He knew that some people needed to grapple with tough questions before they could come to faith in Christ.

A modern-day Paul is Josh McDowell, known worldwide for his ministry to university students. His books, *Evidence That Demands a Verdict* and its sequel *Evidence That Demands a Verdict, Vol. II*, have sold hundreds of thousands of copies and have had a tremendous impact on questioning seekers.

What about you? Could you be an intellectual evangelist? Are you an effective debater? Do you enjoy examining evidence and reasoning through to a conclusion? Do you like to wrestle with difficult questions? Do you love it when cultists come to your door? Then take your calling as an intellectual evangelist seriously. Read, study, and train yourself.

At our church certain staff and lay members naturally approach Christianity from an intellectual standpoint. They have developed a vital ministry by making themselves available to counsel people tripped up by intellectual issues. They've led many people to the Lord as they've patiently answered questions and provided deeper insights.

"He Changed My Life"—Testimonial

The ninth chapter of John records Jesus' healing of a blind beggar. Well-known to the community because of his impertinent begging, the healed man became the center of a controversy.

Neighbors questioned if he really was the same man they'd seen begging since his birth. Pharisees wondered who healed him and questioned the godliness of someone who would heal on the Sabbath. Others concluded that only a sinless man could perform such deeds. Finally they asked the blind man himself what he thought of his healer. His answer was pure and simple, "One thing I do know. I was blind but now I see!" (John 9:25).

His simple testimonial only piqued more controversy, so he expanded his explanation. "Nobody has ever heard of opening the eyes of a man born blind. If this man were not from God, he could do nothing" (John 9:32–33). Draw your own conclusions, he seems to say. I've drawn mine.

Testimonial style evangelists neither confront nor intellectualize. They simply tell the story of the miraculous work of Jesus Christ in their life. They say, "I was spiritually blind, but now I see. Jesus Christ changed my life, and He can change yours."

Testimonial evangelists are usually *not* the people who became Christians as children and followed a steady path of spiritual growth. Typically they have fairly dramatic stories of renewal and transformation. Often they can say things like this: "For the first thirty-two years of my life, I thought I was a Christian because I went to church once in a while and tried to live a moral life. But then a few years back I found out what a real Christian was. I found out I had to trust Jesus Christ as my personal Savior. I did, and it was the best decision I ever made. It revolutionized my life! If you ever want to talk about it more, I'd be happy to."

What happens when seekers hear simple testimonies like that from people they respect? Sometimes nothing happens. Sometimes they say, "That's great for you, Dave. Now can we order our meal?" But sometimes they begin to think. Sometimes they say, "Wait a minute, I thought I was a Christian too—for all those same reasons. I better learn more about this."

In the evangelism seminars at our church we strongly encourage people to write out a brief testimony and become familiar enough with it that they can present it clearly and comfortably. We've found that being prepared with a concise, non-preachy explanation of their conversion frees them to witness effectively in the settings the Holy Spirit orchestrates. Many seekers don't need to hear a sermon; they just need a solid, sane, normal Christian to share with them a slice of their transformed life.

Live It Out—Relational

In Mark 5 we read of a man tormented by an unclean spirit. Living among the tombs, he behaved like a wild man, constantly crying out and gnashing himself with stones. One day Jesus met him and cast the unclean spirit out of him. The man was so overjoyed that he begged Jesus to let him join Him as sort of an itinerant evangelist.

Jesus refused to let him come. He said, "Go home to your family and tell them how much the Lord has done for you, and how he has had mercy on you" (5:19). He told him to be a relational evangelist, one who shares his faith with those he's close to.

Jesus, in effect, said, "Don't go knocking on doors, doing 'cold-turkey' evangelism with people you don't even know. You have family and friends who need to know what I have done in your life. Go home and live a transformed life in their presence. Diligently pray for them, then wait for divinely appointed opportunities to tell your story. Be available when someone says, 'How can I get what you have?'"

Some people put evangelistic blinders on because they can't stand the thought of talking about Christianity with strangers or casual acquaintances. Because of the blinders, they fail to notice the evangelistic opportunities within their existing relationships. Others feel guilty because they can't go to Africa or India and "reach the lost." All the while, God is needing someone just like them to be an evangelist right where they are.

Could that describe you? Do you have friends and family members who don't know the Lord? If so, begin to pour your time, concern, and prayers in their direction. Make yourself available to be God's personal agent to them.

"Come and Hear"—Invitational

Most people are familiar with the story of the Samaritan woman at the well (John 4). After a lengthy conversation with Jesus, she became convinced that He was the Son of God. She excitedly left her water pots and ran into the city. Instead of trying to recreate the conversation in her own words, she begged the people of the city to come to the well and hear Jesus for themselves. They did, and verse 39 tells us that many of the Samaritans believed in Him.

The Samaritan woman was an invitational evangelist. She knew she wasn't prepared to articulate the message in a powerful way. So she invited her friends and acquaintances to come and hear someone who could explain it more effectively.

Many people condemn themselves because they're not confrontational or intellectual. They don't have a dramatic testimony to share. They're not particularly relational. They feel they have nothing to offer as an evangelist. Perhaps God wants them to do just what the woman at the well did: Invite people to "Come and hear."

I asked one of our church members how he came to Christ. He said, "For ten years I was in a searching mode. I was trying to find out what life was all about and what was worth pursuing. I wondered about Christianity. I wondered about Eastern religions. But I didn't know where to turn, and nobody during that ten-year period offered me any help. Then one day I was out jogging. A man from my neighborhood started jogging with me, and when he learned I was new to the area and didn't attend a church, he invited me to visit church with him. I did, and I met Christ. I don't know where I'd be if that man hadn't invited me."

I estimate that fifty percent of the people who write and tell me about their conversion experience say something like this: "I was lost. I was confused. I was lonely. Then someone invited me to a Sunday service—or to a concert, a holiday service, a special event. I kept coming back, and over time I came to know Christ in a personal way."

Periodically our church produces outreach musicals specifically designed to appeal to seekers who aren't yet ready to come to an actual church service. Before our last musical, a woman said to me, "You know, I'm trying my best to fill a row. I can't do evangelism very well, but I can bring my friends to hear music and drama that will point them to Christ. My goal is to fill a row."

Do you think you might be an invitational evangelist? Then get aggressive! Find out about events specifically designed for unbelievers. Find out about Christian concerts and special events. Look for a church that provides opportunities for seekers and new believers. Use the valuable evangelistic style God has given you to make a mark for eternity.

"How Can I Help?"—Serving

One of the most endearing people in Scripture is a woman named Dorcas. She tremendously impacted her city by doing deeds of kindness. She made garments for the poor and forgotten, and distributed them in the name of Christ. She may never have knocked on a door; it's unlikely she ever preached a sermon. Yet through her acts of service she pointed people to the God who could transform human hearts and fill them with love (Acts 9).

Dorcas was a service evangelist. She used her unique serving gifts as tangible expressions of the Gospel message. Like her, you may have a tender spirit and helpful heart. You may have gifts of mercy, helps, hospitality, giving, and counseling. You may be very effective evangelists as you connect sharing Christ with serving people.

I recently received a letter from a person who wrote, "My life was profoundly affected by visiting the food distribution center supported by your church. I had lost hope and went to the food pantry in desperation. The woman who gave me the food said, 'We provide this food because our lives have been changed by Jesus Christ, and we want you to know that you matter to Him.' I'm not a Christian, but I'm thinking about it now. I never knew before that I mattered to God!"

Have you been intimidated by outspoken evangelists who make you feel like a second-class citizen because all you can do is "serve people"? Please don't feel that way. Serve with a joyful, compassionate heart and say, "I offer this service because I want you to know you matter to God." You will plant seeds that others can water and the Holy Spirit can bring to fruition. Be assured. There are many unbelievers who know exactly what they need to do to become a Christian. The one thing they lack is someone like you to soften their heart through your acts of service. Be that person for them!

WHICH LINK ARE YOU?

"A person's coming to Christ is like a chain with many links. There is the first link, middle links, and a last link. There are many influences and conversations that precede a person's decision to convert to Christ. I know the joy of being the first link at times, a middle link usually, and occasionally the last link. God has not called me to only be the last link. He has called me to be faithful and to love all people."[1]

Authentic evangelists know they're just one link in the chain of conversion to Christ. But they also know that every link is important. They know they need to do their part. They need to reach out to the Lord with their personal evangelistic style.

Jesus calls you to enter the people business. He calls you to be a difference-maker for eternity. Will you accept the challenge?

NOTES

1. Cliffe Knechtle, *Give Me an Answer* (Downers Grove, Ill.: InterVarsity Press, 1986), 164.

11

Work: Turning Drudgery to Fulfillment

I can't believe it. Now I can buy a new car, pay off my house—and never work another day in my life!" Multi-million-dollar lottery winners often echo that rendition of everyone's dream. Hollywood paints the fantasy in living color each time it produces a new variation on the old theme: Joe Average falls into enormous wealth and spends his days sipping exotic drinks on a palm-lined Caribbean beach. As the credits roll, we think, "That's what I'd like to do: Quit work and play for the rest of my life."

Many people see work as a necessary evil. They endure the five-day workweek to support the activities of the workless weekend. They lie awake nights, scheming ways to arrange early retirement. Believing God inflicted labor on human beings as a punishment for disobedience, they imagine Him angrily screaming at Adam and Eve, "I'll fix you. From now on, you're doomed to the rock pile of human labor. The best years of your life will be wasted in work, work, work!" In their minds, work becomes a sentence to be served, a penance to be paid, a curse to be endured for as long as necessary.

CURSE OR BLESSING?

The truth is, human labor was no more God's curse than life itself. Though the Fall did lead to consequences that tainted work, we can't forget that God introduced the concept of human labor *before* the Fall. When Adam and Eve were still innocent of sin, God gave them a job to do. He called Adam to name the animals, then asked Adam and Eve to subdue the animals, manage the Garden of Eden, and prepare food from the plants and trees He had provided.

Why would a loving God put His children to work as soon as He created them? Because He knew human labor was a blessing. He knew it would provide them challenges, excitement, adventure, and rewards that nothing else would. He knew that creatures made in His image needed to devote their time to meaningful tasks.

The writer of Ecclesiastes understood this when he wrote, "Then I realized that it is good and proper for a man to eat and drink, and to find satisfaction in his toilsome labor under the sun during the few days of life God has given him—for this is his lot" (Eccl. 5:18). This writer understood that if we have enough to eat and drink, and if we enjoy our work, we are blessed people.

I CAN'T WAIT TO GET TO WORK

Over the years, I've met hundreds of people who can't wait to get up in the morning. I've met people who love being accountants, skilled craftsmen, commodities traders, schoolteachers, bank tellers, house-cleaners, landscapers, hairstylists, mechanics, and every other kind of worker imaginable. And the vitality and enthusiasm generated by their love for their work affects positively their whole life. It spills over into their marriages, parenting, friendships, and recreational pursuits.

On the other hand, I've met hundreds of people whose dissatisfaction with their jobs casts a shadow over every other dimension of life. They may earn the same money, enjoy the same prestige, and have the same job description as their satisfied counterparts, but they're unhappy and frustrated. They take out their unhappiness on the kids and the dog, and they walk through life in a haze of bitterness and lethargy. They can't wait to throw off the weight of their labors.

What causes the difference? Why can two people share the same job, and one be joy-filled and energetic, while the other is unhappy and drained?

The key is vocational authenticity, which means we have the right job, for the right reason, and enjoy the right rewards.

WHAT TURNS YOUR CRANK?

Almost all satisfied workers share one thing in common: They labor in the field of their motivated abilities. They do work that is consistent with their God-given abilities, talents, and interest.

Motivated abilities often appear in early childhood play. Some children have a natural aptitude for building things. In their hands simple blocks become architectural wonders and construction sets open a world of discovery. Other children find fascination in words and fill every quiet moment with books. Some spend free time on science projects. Still others gravitate naturally to athletics, or the arts.

Some children enjoy playing alone, while others have to "invite a friend over" the minute they get home from school. Some emerge as natural leaders, and others are perfectly content to follow.

Perceptive parents can often pick up hints about possible vocational pursuits in the way their children play. Wise parents will encourage their children in those directions. It's not uncommon for satisfied workers to look back and see the seeds of their job success in their youthful recreational choices and extracurricular pursuits.

When I was in youth ministry, one high school student emerged as an unusually gifted leader. When we divided the youth group into subgroups called teams, his team always developed the strongest identity and attracted the greatest number of new kids. He seemed to have a special knack for organizing, inspiring, and leading others. Today he's on the management team at our church, overseeing nearly one hundred members of our pastoral staff. He's an extremely effective manager because his responsibilities are consistent with his God-given abilities.

Our director of programming also grew up in our youth group and also exhibited her natural aptitudes at an early age. In grade school she staged plays and musicals in her basement, taking shades off lamps to make spotlights, rearranging furniture to design sets, and raiding closets to create one-of-a-kind costumes. Then she invited neighbor kids to come and watch. In high school, instead of being *in* the school variety shows, she *produced* them. In college, she studied the communication arts. Now she coordinates the music, drama, media, and production departments at our church and is responsible for programming our midweek and weekend services.

I know a salesman who could sell ice to an Eskimo, sand to a Bedouin, or anything to a Dutchman. (Being Dutch, I know what a challenge that is.) He describes himself as a kid who enjoyed highly social kinds of play, loved competition, and was always the life of the party. He was easily bored and needed constant challenge and stimulation. He was never happier than when he sold his sister's Girl Scout cookies door to door! Is it any wonder he's a successful salesman today?

But let's take that same relational, competitive, high-energy little guy, roll the years ahead, and make him the assistant librarian in the township library. How would you predict his job satisfaction level? I think he would last about two weeks—even if the job offered great pay and unbelievable perks. It wouldn't meet his need for action, competition, and variety. It wouldn't be in sync with his motivated abilities.

The same thing would happen if we put a more introverted, reserved person on the front line of a Broadway production, or made him the guest host on *Saturday Night Live*. With tremendous effort he might pull it off, but he'd hate every minute of it. From the job satisfaction standpoint, it would be an unmitigated disaster.

God intends our work to be a natural expression of who we are, consistent with our inherent interests and abilities. When it isn't, we feel out of place, insignificant, and either bored or defeated. When it is, we feel like we have something important to contribute, and we're challenged without being overwhelmed.

My daughter loves to sing and dance and act. Recently she performed in a musical production. As I tucked her into bed that night, she said, "You know, Dad, I feel like I really come to life when I'm singing and dancing. That's when I *live*." God wants each of us to have that kind of response to our life's work. He wants our labors to energize us and pump vitality into our daily lives.

Does yours? Is it consistent with your God-given uniqueness and your motivated abilities? If you can't answer yes, or if you've never identified your motivated abilities, please visit a career counselor, take a vocational aptitude test, or read one of the excellent books on this subject. Two books I suggest are *Finding a Job You Can Love* by Ralph Mattson and Arthur Miller from Thomas Nelson Publishers and *The*

1988 *What Color Is Your Parachute?* by Richard Nelson Bolles from Ten Speed Press.[1]

Before deciding on a career, everyone ought to answer the "What turns your crank?" question. When we interview prospective church employees, we put it this way: "If you could wave a wand and write your own job description, what would you write? What do you love to do more than anything else? What do you feel you're best at? How do you like to spend your vocational time?" We know that if we can shape a position closely consistent with those natural desires, we'll have an enthusiastic, satisfied, effective worker.

Extenuating circumstances sometimes force us to settle for jobs outside our range of interests and strengths, but to the extent we can, we should view them as temporary. God wants each of us to enjoy vocational authenticity, which begins with having a job consistent with our God-given motivated abilities.

AS FOR THE LORD

The second requirement for an authentic job life is that we do our work for the right reason: to please and glorify God. When a Christian walks on the job site he should be thinking about more than making money, impressing the boss, or even how much he enjoys his work. He should be conjuring up ways to honor God through his marketplace endeavors.

Colossians 3:23–24 says, "Whatever you do, work at it with all your heart, as working for the Lord, not for men, since you know that you will receive an inheritance from the Lord as a reward. It is the Lord Christ you are serving."

Wherever we work, whatever our job description, our ultimate boss is Jesus Christ. He's the one we need to please. When we do, our work becomes a source of worship. Our job site becomes a temple. Each project we undertake becomes an offering to God.

But how do we do that? How do we honor God in the marketplace?

How We Work

We honor God, first, by being credible workers. By striving for excellence. By earning a reputation for diligence, thoroughness, and conscientiousness. By making significant contributions to the work team.

When I was chaplain for the Chicago Bears, I often heard behind-the-scenes analyses of various players. Players had little use for teammates who slacked off in practice, gave less than one hundred percent during games, were publicity hounds, or seemed more concerned about money than the good of the team. Such players who claimed to be Christians dishonored the name of Christ.

It should never be said of Christian workers that they are halfhearted, careless, tardy, irresponsible, whiny, or negligent. Behavior like that embarrasses God. It brings reproach on Him.

Christian workers should epitomize character qualities like self-discipline, perseverance, and initiative. They should be self-motivated, prompt, organized, and industrious. Their efforts should result in work of the very highest quality.

Why? Because they're not just laying bricks; they're building a wall for God's glory. They're not just teaching a class; they're educating young students for God's glory. They're not just balancing the books; they're keeping the ledgers in excellent order for God's glory. They're not just driving a tractor; they're plowing a straight furrow for God's glory.

Again, Paul tells us to do our work "with all our hearts"—with energy and excellence. That's the first step in honoring God in our work.

Who We Are

Once we've established ourselves as valuable assets and credible workers, then we're free to honor God on a more personal level: by who we are and how we behave in marketplace relationships.

It goes without saying that Christians must exhibit personal integrity in the marketplace. We must shun, without exception, unethical business practices and financial improprieties, even violations as commonplace as making unauthorized calls on business phones or being careless with expense accounts. Christians must strive every day to be beyond reproach in all their marketplace dealings and practices.

But that's only the beginning. To really honor God by who we are, Christian workers need to conscientiously model a marketplace lifestyle directly opposed to the typical standard.

Generally speaking, marketplace mentality centers solely on the bottom line: profits, quotas, sales reports, balance sheets, budgets, and competition. The goal is to pump out more work in less time with lower costs. In an environment like that, people become the lowest priority.

Yet the marketplace cries out for humanness and compassion, for the touch of Christlikeness. Who better can provide that than Christian men and women who have experienced divine love and been transformed by divine power?

Yet too often Christian workers get caught up in the same self-seeking mentality that snares unbelievers. Pretty soon they too relegate other people to low priority status. They become robotlike in their encounters and superficial in their conversations. They no longer take time to offer compliments and affirmation, or respond to needs, or express interest in coworkers' personal lives.

Eventually coworkers get the message: "Christians are just like everybody else—more interested in profits than people; more concerned about themselves than others."

It is alarmingly easy for sincere believers to slip into self-centeredness. I know. Time and again I've gotten so consumed with message preparation or administrative responsibilities that I've passed a staff member in the hallway, glimpsed a look of pain or frustration, and walked on, telling myself I was too busy to respond. "Hope he works it out," I'd think. "Hope someone can help her." Often I've been chastised by the inner voice of the Holy Spirit: "Who do you think you are? Where is the likeness of Christ I ought to see in you? Have you forgotten what's really important?"

Marketplace mentality is notoriously self-centered and survivalistic. Christians have the opportunity to mark the marketplace by overturning that modus operandi, by acting like brothers and sisters to their coworkers rather than like cutthroat competitors.

Philippians 2:4 says, "Each of you should look not only to your own interests, but also to the interests of others." In the marketplace that means we need to *make* time to express interest in others—in their spouse, kids, health, problems, goals, frustrations, hobbies, vacations, and dreams. Competitors don't care about those things, but brothers and sisters do.

We also need to be helpers in the marketplace. That may mean offering to take up slack in another worker's load. It may mean staying late to help a partner finish a report, or occasionally working through lunch to help someone meet a deadline.

Honoring God also requires Christians to be vulnerable in the marketplace. That means admitting to wrongdoing, and saying, "Look,

I was feeling pressed and I took it out on you. I said things I shouldn't have. I'm sorry. Please forgive me. I'm trying to overcome that problem." Let's face it. Even the most devout Christian is going to "botch it" now and then. We're going to make mistakes, use poor judgment, lose our tempers, speak unkindly about someone, and fail to meet work standards.

The important question is: What do we do then? Do we try to rationalize misbehavior? Do we throw the blame on someone else? Do we cover up?

Contrary to what many Christians think, we do not have to be perfect to have integrity with unbelievers. We don't have to be plastic caricatures with painted smiles. We need to be human, sincere, honest, transparent, humble—real people who make mistakes, admit them, and then move on.

We honor God by being genuinely interested, by being helpers, by being vulnerable, and finally, by being reconcilers. More doors have been slammed, names called, and conversations coldly terminated in the marketplace than anywhere else. Rampant relational breakdown is almost a given. Christians honor God by entering that relational war zone as agents of reconciliation. That doesn't mean they avoid conflict. It means they apply the principles of relational authenticity. They enter the tunnel of chaos, and even lead others there when necessary, knowing that openly dealing with hostility and misunderstanding is the only path to harmony.

In a milieu increasingly known for its impersonality and blatantly self-serving mentality, Christians have the opportunity to honor God by upholding a different code. Will it be a challenge? Will it sometimes meet resistance? Will it require sacrifices of time? Will it occasionally force Christians to lose the competitive edge? Will commitment to ethical practices sometimes mean fewer customers, lower profits, perhaps even job loss?

Yes, to all those questions. Honoring God by who you are in the marketplace is no easy task. It demands a radical flip-flop of values, and a die-hard determination to row upstream. But it offers the potential to bring the impact of integrity and the touch of compassion to an environment often devoid of both. It also opens the door to a third means of honoring God in the marketplace.

What We Say

Once we earn credibility by how we work and who we are, we then become free to make an *eternal* impact in our workaday world by what we say. We can be spokespersons who've earned the right to be heard, agents of divine change, missionaries to the marketplace.

How do we start?

By praying for divinely appointed opportunities to put our personal evangelistic styles to work. For some that will mean going out for lunch and sharing with their coworkers the stories of their conversions. For others it will mean extending mercy to a sick colleague—covering for the person at work, preparing a hot meal and delivering it at home, sending flowers or a gift of encouragement—and writing a simple note saying, "God has been so gracious to me. I just wanted to share some of His love with you." Others will buy tickets to a Christian concert and offer them to coworkers, or invite them to church and to their house for Sunday brunch. Still others will be led by the Spirit to confront coworkers with the futility of their pursuits and their need for a genuine encounter with Jesus Christ.

Christians have often been ineffective in their attempts to make eternal impact because they've neglected the first two steps in honoring God in the marketplace. They've been careless workers whose shoddy methods and inferior standards offended coworkers. Or they've been inconsistent Christians whose behavior was shaped more by marketplace mindset than the mind of Christ. In either case, they've forfeited their credibility and turned an opportunity into a closed door.

What a shame! For eight hours a day, five days a week, Christians rub shoulders with men and women who matter to God and desperately need to hear more about Him. Paul aptly wrote, "How can they believe in the one of whom they have not heard? And how can they hear without someone preaching to them?" (Rom. 10:14). At work we can be that "someone" who can tell them.

Jesus never commanded us to engage in theological debates with strangers, flaunt four-inch crosses and Jesus stickers, or throw out Christian catchphrases. But He did tell us to work and live in such a way that when the Holy Spirit orchestrates opportunities to speak about God, we will have earned the right.

RIGHT REWARDS

Vocational authenticity means we pursue the right job (in line with our motivated abilities), for the right reason (to honor God), and finally, that we enjoy the right rewards.

Confidence

Have you ever been served in a restaurant by a brand new waiter or waitress? You can usually tell by their obvious nervousness and awkwardness. They often spill water and deliver food in a clumsy, disorganized fashion. And they tend to be either preoccupied and unavailable, or overly solicitous and bothersome.

But if you happen to see them two weeks later, you'll likely see an amazing transformation. Gone is the self-conscious nervousness. They adroitly balance four plates of food and a drinks platter, while they weave their way between crowded tables and banter freely with pleased patrons. Their motions are fluid, their manner comfortable, and they radiate a sense of healthy confidence.

That's one of the rewards of vocational authenticity. Confidence. It develops in our lives when we accept marketplace challenges and stretch our abilities.

Once I questioned the concrete contractor working on our church addition about the rash of construction accidents I'd heard about recently. He looked me square in the eye and said, "You don't have to worry about that here, *Son*. I've been pouring concrete foundations since before you were born. I poured my first concrete wall in 1946 and it's still standing tall and strong. This building will be no problem."

Confidence in one's competence is a blessing of incalculable worth. What better place to develop it than the marketplace?

One of the most confident leaders in biblical history was King David. He was a self-assured leader, soldier, and statesman. Scripture gives some clues about how he developed that confidence. When he was just a small child, he was a shepherd. That meant he had to roam the countryside night and day, alone, to seek pastures and water for his sheep. All the while, he had to scan the hillsides to make sure no wild animals were lurking about. Scripture says that once a bear threatened the sheep, and David attacked and killed it. Later he did the same thing to a lion.

When the need arose for a warrior to face the famed Goliath, David volunteered, citing his past success in defeating the bear and lion. When he became king, he overcame enemy armies and led Israel into its golden era.

Where did David get the confidence to be such a strong and able leader? I think the seeds were sown on the hillsides of Palestine, when he took his first job as a shepherd boy.

Few arenas make as rigorous demands on us as does the marketplace. It says, "Here's a challenge. It's up to you. Start in. Learn. Grow. Work hard. Get the job done." When we start we feel uncomfortable and fearful. But as we become increasingly proficient in our tasks, those unpleasant sensations are gradually replaced by a satisfying sense of confidence. Almost without our realizing it, we begin thinking thoughts like these: "God has given me gifts and abilities and talents. I have strengths and valuable skills. I'm a competent person. I have something to offer this company. I can do excellent work. I'm an important member of the team."

Those moments of positive self-awareness are exactly what God had in mind for us to experience in the marketplace. God gave us abilities to invest in meaningful labor, in part, so we could receive the rich reward of self-confidence.

Lottery winners often find that lying on the beach is not all it's cracked up to be. God instituted human labor because He knew our confidence and self-esteem would soar, not in the ease of long-term leisure, but in the pursuit of meaningful labor.

Character Development

The second reward of diligent labor is improved character. I can easily trace the development of my greatest character strengths back to the years when I worked in the family wholesale produce business.

My dad loved to work. And he loved to put his kids to work. When I was in grade school, he'd wake me up at 5:00 A.M. and take me to the warehouse to unload semis filled with produce that needed to be distributed to local hospitals, restaurants, and grocery stores.

On more than one occasion, after an hour or two hauling cases of oranges, tomatoes, or lettuce, I would jump down from the trailer to take a break, only to have Dad see me and ask, "Is that truck all unloaded? If it isn't, get back there and finish the job."

Later he put me to work on company farms, planting and harvesting seed. During the crucial planting weeks we would work from early morning to late at night. Sometimes in the middle of a burning afternoon, I'd cruise by the barn to refuel the tractor and ask if

I could take a couple hours off and go water-skiing with my friends. He'd say, "Are you finished with the field? If not, get back to work. Finish the job, Son!"

At the time I thought many of his requests were unreasonable. I hated it when he said, "Finish the job." I thought his work ethic was way overdone! Now, more than ten years after his death, I thank God almost every day for using my dad and the marketplace to burn certain character qualities in my life. There's a lot I lack in terms of natural ability and raw potential. But one thing I have in spades is the character quality of perseverance. I know how to finish the job.

What's great is that, like confidence, character improvements spill over into other areas of life. If I get frustrated in working through a relational difficulty, part of me says, "Give up. Take a break. It's not worth it." But another part says, "Keep trying. Pursue reconciliation. Finish the job."

If I'm struggling with my relationship with God, unaware of His presence and uninspired in my attempts to journal and pray, part of me says, "Forget it. Try again tomorrow. It's not worth the effort." But another part of me says, "Keep pursuing. Keep listening. Finish the job."

The marketplace affords us the opportunity to develop every character quality God wants us to have. Are you enrolled in the marketplace classroom of character development? Do you look for opportunities on the job to practice godly virtues?

When you get bogged down in a frustrating assignment, do you give up or do you see it as a chance to grow in perseverance? When tempted by an unethical practice, do you yield or do you see it as a chance to grow in honesty? When you hear a friend being slandered, do you give silent assent, or do you stand up for your friend and practice loyalty? When you become irritated by a coworker's idiosyncrasies, do you criticize and belittle him, or do you commit yourself to learning greater tolerance? When you're asked to stretch in an area of weakness, do you let fear stop you, or do you decide to muster courage and proceed?

The marketplace can provide graduate-level instruction in character development that can transform our lives and free us to be the men and women God wants us to be. It's up to us to use the opportunity and learn the lessons. Many people throw it away, but those who take advantage of it enjoy the unexpected reward of personal growth and maturity.

Feeling of Accomplishment

When God completed His creative endeavors, He paused, looked over His handiwork, and said, "Behold! This is very good." Oozing from that divine statement is the blessed feeling of accomplishment. It's as though God were saying, "I conceived of this idea, I started the job, I stuck with it, I finished it, and I did it well." There's fulfillment in the completion of diligent labor.

I think part of the appeal of the best-selling book, *Iacocca,* was Lee's picture on the front cover. He's leaning back in the leather chair in his office, cupping his hands behind his head, flashing his infectious smile. His demeanor effuses the satisfaction of accomplishment. You can almost read his thoughts. "I made a high-risk play. I accepted the challenge. I faced the adventure. I endured the difficulty. I beat the odds. I turned Chrysler around. And I feel *great!*"

Meaningful labor gives each of us the opportunity to enjoy the blessing of accomplishment. It provides a sweet reward to the salesman who closes the deal and silently screams, "I did it!"; to the janitor who puts away the cleaning equipment and surveys an immaculate facility; to the teacher who finishes the last lecture; to the farmer who harvests the last row; to the soprano who sings the last note of the concert; to the accountant who balances the last ledger; to the athlete who showers and leaves the stadium; to the architect who finishes the final drawings; to the mother who finally puts the baby down for the night; to the student who completes the final exam.

All of those moments are precious slices of reality reserved for people who labor diligently. When we engage in work that taps our God-given abilities, and when we do it to the best of our ability for God's honor, then we enjoy those blessed moments of accomplishment. And nothing beats that! I'm all for leisure-time activities, vacations, diversions, and breaks. They bring much-needed balance and sanity to our lives. But their greatest value is that they refresh us so we can resume our labors with greater energy, effectiveness, and creativity—and know greater accomplishment.

Human labor was designed by God, assigned to every one of us, and offered as an opportunity to build confidence, develop character, and enjoy the satisfaction of accomplishment. Does that sound like a curse?

Vocational authenticity, where we have the right job, for the right reason, and enjoy the right rewards, allows us to experience labor as the blessing it was meant to be.

ADDICTED!

Unfortunately, the blessing becomes a curse to those who allow their professions to become obsessions. Some people develop a psychological addiction to their work that causes them to alienate family and friends, neglect their health, and sabotage their spiritual lives. Though they seldom admit that work is their god, it's obvious to others. Their job is what they live for, what they dream of, what they sacrifice all else for. For them the blessing of human labor becomes what the next drink is to the alcoholic.

Why do workaholics work too much, play too little, and allow their personal lives to disintegrate? Some assume the motivation is simple greed; they want more money. Others believe workaholics just love their jobs more than other people do. They overdose on job satisfaction. Still others think it's purely a function of temperament type: Certain types are naturally driven to overwork.

In reality, the driving force for most workaholics is personal insecurity. Certainly there are exceptions to this rule, but many workaholics have low self-esteem and a crying need for approval. Deep inside they feel like losers, and because they hate that feeling, they decide to do whatever it takes to prove they're winners. They sacrifice everything—health, marriage, kids, sometimes their very soul—to prove they're a Somebody. They believe that if they can be impressive, powerful, and wealthy, they'll earn others' respect, and eventually feel good about themselves. This may be a subconscious drive, but it's as powerful as an addictive drug.

Many workaholics grew up in homes where love and acceptance had to be earned by accomplishing tangible objectives. Because their love need was so strong, they pushed themselves unmercifully to produce, compete, and excel. As they grew older, they continued the pattern in an ongoing attempt to procure love.

Others grew up in homes where alcoholism, parental death, or marital breakdown created an environment short on affection and warmth. This left them with an unmet longing to experience affection, to know they were treasured and appreciated, to feel like they mattered to someone. Thus they go through their adult lives striving— through their performance—to buy words of affirmation and approval.

AN UNBREAKABLE CYCLE

Recently I learned of a man who worked so hard to build his company that his wife and children were on the point of leaving and his health was deteriorating. In desperation, he sold his company and bought a small-time marina on a beautiful lake. The family was delighted at the prospect of working together in a slow-paced family operation.

But the change in geography didn't change the man's need to prove himself. Within five years he transformed the run-down marina into a multi-million dollar enterprise, the most innovative venture of its kind. A friend of mine spoke to him. "You must feel very proud every time you see that marina. It's a tremendous accomplishment." The man said, "No, every time I see it, I feel sick to my stomach. That marina has cost me *everything*."

It had. During the miraculous transformation of the marina, his wife and kids had lost hope and left him. His spiritual pursuits floundered in the abyss of overscheduling. And his body had succumbed to the heart disease that eventually took his life.

Did he want to break out of the cycle of overwork? Yes. But his deep insecurity drove him to repeat the same mistakes he had made before. In the end he lost everything.

FREED BY LOVE

Jesus asked a group of first-century workaholics how smart it was to gain the whole world and lose their very souls. How smart was it to win an insignificant race, and lose the real race? How smart was it to put everything in one little battle, and lose the war?

These are sobering realities that strike at the heart of every workaholic. They force him or her to ask, "What can I do to get off the treadmill? How can I break the force of the drive? How can I withstand the pressure?"

The answer is simple but profound: Workaholics have to be loved like they have never been loved before. They need to be affirmed, approved, treasured—even spoiled! Who can do that for them? Our God.

I'm not saying that mere intellectual understanding of God's love will free workaholics. They need to experience personally the purity and fullness of God's love. On an emotional level they need to grasp the fact that they can't earn God's favor; they can only accept it as a free and unmerited gift. When workaholics experience the tender touch of God's love, and the cleansing, forgiveness, and acceptance that accompany salvation, then they can become free from the bondage of workaholism. Resting in the security of God's love will help them become less driven to impress others through their marketplace achievements.

In addition to internalizing this spiritual understanding, workaholics need to take practical steps to break the bad habits associated with workaholism. First, they need to limit the number of hours they spend at their job. This doesn't mean they "try" to leave the job site a little earlier. It means they decide on a set number of hours they'll work, then stick with that commitment. If they can't do it on their own, they need to have others hold them accountable.

It's no secret that I have wrestled with the disease of workaholism. Earlier in my ministry, I found it impossible to leave the office on time. There was enough work to keep me busy around the clock, and it nearly did. When I finally experienced a change of heart, I decided that nine and a half hours at work was my daily limit. Then I asked a few close friends to check up on me and make sure I left the office at the appointed time. Naturally I had to delegate certain responsibilities and formulate a more realistic job description.

Second, workaholics recovering from their addiction need to set aside predetermined times to invest in marriage and family life. When I decided to modify my schedule, I determined that with the responsibilities of a home, a wife, and two young children, I had to be home four nights a week—not home in body only, with my mind preoccupied with ministry, but fully engaged in the lives of my wife and children. I decided that was what it would take for me to be a godly husband and father. I still maintain that commitment, and if I end up short one week, I make up for it with extra time the next.

Third, workaholics need to plan breaks and vacations in advance—and take them! Workaholics are notorious for saying, "I'll break away when I get the chance." But they never do. I once talked to a man who claimed he hadn't taken a vacation in twenty years. I wasn't surprised; I had already met his wounded wife and kids. His workaholism was written all over their faces.

Finally, the workaholic must learn how to say "No!" to that which would feed his illness. No to more work opportunities, more deals, more engagements, more appointments. Nonworkaholics can't possibly understand how hard it is for workaholics to say no to opportunities to enhance their impressiveness. They need help from spouses, friends, perhaps even counselors. One workaholic I know checks out every new opportunity with her accountability group. That is the only way she can keep from making unhealthy commitments.

Human labor is a blessing, but only when it takes its rightful place and is carefully balanced with spiritual, relational, recreational, and physical demands.

IT'S WHAT WE MAKE IT!

For most of us, the vast majority of our time is devoted to work. That's why it's so important to experience vocational authenticity.

If your job is drudgery because it's not in line with your natural abilities, pray for self-understanding and begin to pursue career options. If you're failing to honor God by how you work and behave in the marketplace, confess your sin and pray for the courage to be a genuine man or woman of God. If you're not enjoying the rewards of meaningful labor, step out in faith. Try something new that stretches your abilities. Accept a challenge that will tap your potential and promote a sense of accomplishment.

If personal insecurity has caused your work to become an obsession, memorize these words from Isaiah 43: "Fear not, for I have redeemed you; I have summoned you by name; you are mine. You are precious and honored in my sight . . . I love you." Immerse yourself in Scripture, books, and tapes that affirm God's love for you. Then take practical steps to break the habits of workaholism.

Human labor. A curse or a blessing? It's what we make it.

NOTES

1. Other good books in this area include *The Quick Job Hunting Map/A Fast Way to Help* and *The Three Boxes of Life* by Richard N. Bolles; *Finding Work* by James Bramlett; *Get That Job* and *How to Get a Job in Chicago* by Thomas M. Camden; *The Complete Job Search Handbook* by Howard Figler; *Getting to Yes: Negotiating Agreement Without Giving In* by Roger Fisher and William Ury; *The Robert Half Way to Get Hired in Today's Job Market* by Robert Half; *Christians in the Marketplace* by Bill Hybels; *Get the Salary You Want* by Marilyn M. Kennedy; *The Job Hunters' Handbook/A Christian Guide* by Rodney S. Laughlin; *Sweaty Palms* by Anthony H. Medley; *Parting Company* by William J. Morin and James C. Cabrera; *Getting a Job/A Guide for Choosing a Career* by Michael Pountney; *Passages* by Gail Sheehy.

12

The Seduction of Money

Ⅰt beckons and woos us. It tantalizes and seduces us. It sucks us into its grasp and wreaks havoc in our lives. And still we deny its sinister power.

A Money Monster? Ha! There's no such thing!

Like children proud to have outgrown their belief in nocturnal bedroom threats, we laugh off the notion of a Money Monster. A sinister power? A tyrannizing force? You've got to be kidding! Money is simply a means of exchange.

Meanwhile, we devote our lives to earning it, glory in spending it, and lie awake nights figuring out how to stockpile more of it. We pursue inauthentic jobs because of it. We bow at its feet and salute its command.

There's a Money Monster all right, sly and artful. He's been around for centuries, but during the last twenty years he's moved from the shadows into the mainstream of American life.

In 1967 college freshmen were asked whether it was more important to be well-off financially or to discover a meaningful philosophy of life. The vast majority polled chose a meaningful philosophy of life. In a similar 1986 poll, eighty percent responded that it was more important to be well-off financially.[1] The Monster had been busy.

From 1980 to 1987 the circulation of *Money* magazine doubled. *Lifestyles of the Rich and Famous* made its television debut. Heroes like Martin Luther King and Robert Kennedy gave way to Iacocca, Trump, and Icahn. Business school applications skyrocketed while schools of social work almost shut their doors. Lottery participation soared off the charts. And young people unashamedly sang along to Madonna's hit, "Material Girl."

What's fascinating is that as our financial needs are supplied, our appetite for money tends to increase rather than diminish. When we're physically hungry, we fill our stomachs, then back away from the table. Not so with money. It seems the more we get, the more we want.

When I left the family business to enter the ministry, I turned down a golden opportunity for affluence. I say that with no credit to myself. I felt God's call so definitely that I simply could not refuse. For two years I ministered with no salary. Lynne taught music lessons and we took in boarders to cover the rent. Then I began receiving thirty-five dollars a week, and later eighty-five. We were thrilled!

Eventually our salary was set at twelve thousand dollars a year. I remember thinking, "Who would ever want more than twelve thousand dollars a year?" Soon I found the answer. Me.

As the church grew and my job description enlarged, the board of directors periodically increased my salary. Each time I thought, "Wow, this is far more than I need. Who would ever want more than this?" Twelve months later, I would find out. Me.

Finally in a late night truth-telling session I came to grips with an ugly reality. The more I had, the more I wanted. I'd been believing the Money Monster's lie that just a little bit more would be enough. But when would the drive to accumulate stop? Lynne and I decided then and there to cap my salary. The board agreed to our request, and helped us strike a deadly blow to the Money Monster.

POLITELY REFUSING GOD

The courts of spiritual bankruptcy are filled with men and women who vowed to get serious about their spiritual lives after one more deal, after one more increase, after one more level, after one more . . . more . . . more.

Vast numbers have gained the whole world only to lose their

souls, because they believed the Money Monster's lies. Even sincere Christians have been lured by riches and the love of money; they have squandered their lives and given up their spiritual fruitfulness.

The Money Monster's goal is total domination of our value system without our being aware of it. Unfortunately, we make it fairly easy for him to do that. Consider Michael, a typical American child. During the most impressionable years of his life, he hears a steady stream of dinner table conversations centered almost exclusively on money and the things it can buy. It becomes clear to him at a young age that what Mom and Dad really value is money.

Over the next few years, the family moves several times because of promotions and salary increases. That convinces the perceptive child that monetary increases are more important than establishing stable relational or spiritual roots.

Later on, conversations turn to college, and the dialogue focuses on what professions pay the most rather than what would best suit the young person's motivated abilities. The apparent message is that financial remuneration will make up for lack of job fulfillment.

He eventually enters the job market, taking the position with the highest earning potential, yet always watching for an even better opportunity. On and on it goes, each major life decision being made on the basis of the bottom line. In time our typical American learns to equate his self-worth with his net worth; he judges others by the same standard. He eventually reaches old age, totally unaware that he's been led through life on a leash controlled by the Money Monster.

We all know the story of the rich young ruler (Luke 18:18–30). Jesus' point in that story was that the young man would not be free to follow Him as long as he remained chained to the Money Monster. But the man was so dominated by the sinister power that he politely refused eternal life.

We shake our heads in disbelief. Yet how many times have we similarly rejected a leading from God? A wonderful service opportunity comes our way, but before we say yes our mental calculators start crunching numbers. When the dollar total registers, the leash pulls tightly around our neck, and we say, "Ah, thanks God, but not this time. It'll cost me money. It'll decrease my net worth. I'd have to part with something. I can't, Lord. Not now. Maybe next time."

BUY NOW, PAY LATER

We must be less naive regarding the Money Monster. He's alive and well and pulling out all the stops to get us under his control. He craftily offers his most lethal ploy as the harmless solution to all our financial woes. What is this deadly trap? Easy credit.

Never before has a culture been so committed to the buy now, pay later philosophy. Bumper stickers used to read, "It may not be much, but at least it's paid for." Now flashy imports sport this message, "I owe, I owe, so off to work I go!" I recently saw a bumper sticker in San Diego that said, "I want it all, and I want it now." For too many people, the key to having it all now is easy credit.

My introduction to this mentality came when I was about seven. I was riding with my dad in his pick-up truck, and we passed a farmhouse with a beautiful new luxury car in the driveway. It was white with a vinyl top and had wire wheel covers. It literally glistened in the sun. I said, "Look, Dad. That farmer must be really *rich*." He smiled and said, "Billy, that man is nearly busted. He owes money to everyone in this county, including me." I remember thinking, "That man is goofed up! Why would he buy a car he can't afford?"

As if reading my mind, Dad began an informal lecture frequently given in Dutch homes. "Here's the problem with people today, Billy. They tend to spend more money than they earn. Let's say a young fellow gets a job and makes a down payment on a new Volkswagen. He can barely afford the monthly payments, but he's convinced he needs that car.

"Two years later he gets a raise, but instead of paying off his Volkswagen, he trades it in on a Ford convertible. Now, he's deeper in debt and his monthly payments are even higher, but at least he's having fun in his convertible. After two more years, he gets another raise. This time he trades his convertible in for a luxury model. Now he owes a ton of money and the monthly payments have gone through the roof! But all that matters to him is that he's driving a Lincoln. That's the problem with people today, Billy."

Unfortunately, few people today listen to homespun wisdom like that. Deceptive advertising feeds the belief that we can charge to the hilt and not get caught. An ad for a recent car promotion said, "No money down and no payments for three months." The buyer is almost lulled into believing the car is free—until he gets a payment book as thick as his Bible.

It used to be necessary to qualify for credit cards. Now the average person receives a steady stream of these plastic people-eaters in the mail. What happens? Buyers become enslaved to them. A woman once came to me in abject despair because she'd just learned she couldn't use Visa to pay off Master Card.

Proverbs 22:7 says, "The borrower is servant to the lender." It's true. Pay-later schemes and credit cards have led hundreds of thousands of sincere Christians into financial bondage. And it destroys them! Some of the most anxious people I know are people who have slid down the icy slope of overspending into the deep, cold valley of debt. Now they're shivering at the bottom of the valley, realizing it may take months or years to regain a position of solvency. They never intended to end up in that valley; they're not bad people. They just got sucked into the lure of easy credit.

WHO ARE YOU COPYING?

Why do people spend more than they have? Usually because they're trying to emulate someone else's lifestyle.

The "keeping-up-with-the-Joneses" complex is rarely a consciously competitive activity. It's a subtle pressure that gradually wears down one's discipline and slowly chips away at one's resolve. "If my friends have it all, why can't I? Why am I so committed to my budget? Maybe I can loosen up a bit and incur a little debt like everyone else. I won't lose control."

Issues of self-esteem prod us on. "I'm every bit as talented—or aggressive, educated, competent—as he is. Why shouldn't I have what he has?"

The media feeds our propensity for self-indulgence. Hour after hour, television invites us into the glitz and glamour of affluent lifestyles. I wish someone would study the correlation between hours of television watched and dollars of indebtedness incurred. It's almost unfair. Millions of dollars are spent by advertisers to determine the most effective way to trigger our spending fingers. Top scriptwriters, actors and actresses, musicians, and production people combine forces to get us to do one thing . . . spend money.

We see designer wardrobes that transform physiques and turn heads. We see jewelry that promises to seal love for eternity. We see shiny cars flying through clouds and glistening on majestic mountaintops.

Add to peer pressure and media influence our inherent greed and tendency toward self-indulgence, and it's easy to see why we spend too much. Constantly we're tempted to live beyond our means, and the Money Monster makes sure we give in.

That's not what God wants for us. God wants us to experience financial authenticity. He wants us to *control our money* rather than let *our money control us.* He wants us to be free from indebtedness and the fear that one unexpected expense could sink our ship. He wants us to live within our means and have future expenditures planned for. He wants us to have ample funds to share with those in need. In short, He wants us to master the Money Monster.

WHAT'S YOUR CENTRAL REALITY?

The first step in breaking the sinister power of money is to pursue a more vital relationship with Jesus Christ. People who walk with Him on a consistent, daily basis make an amazing discovery: He satisfies their soul at its deepest level. As they experience this, they find less and less need to ease the pain in their souls with the temporary anesthetics money can buy. They're less obsessed with expensive clothes, luxury cars, and exotic vacations.

Jesus said, "No one can serve two masters. . . . You cannot serve both God and money" (Matt. 6:24). In other words, we cannot have two central values in our life. Either a relationship with Jesus Christ is our central value, or material gain is. We can't bow down at both altars.

The question we need to ask is: which god is worth our ultimate allegiance? Many people think, "If only I had a bigger house, a newer car, a longer vacation . . . then I'd be satisfied." I recently met a millionaire who'd achieved all his financial goals by the age of forty-two. Then he experienced "success panic." He sat in his condo in Palm Springs and suddenly realized that his long list of acquisitions didn't satisfy.

If our central value is the acquisition of material goods, we'll have a hard time living within our means, because we'll never satiate our hunger for more. But material gain never delivers what it promises. Whether we know it or not, what we're really after is *soul* satisfaction. And no home, car, toy, or bank account can provide that.

A secular writer in *Forbes* magazine wrote this: "Sooner or later I expect Americans to give up their comic faith in the miraculous power of money. Not for any preacher's reason, but because, as with any other neurosis, more people will come to appreciate that the substitution of shadow for substance, of illusion for reality, results in behavior both idiotic and dangerous."[2] When, he asks, will Americans wake up to the fact that money doesn't deliver what it promises?

WHAT'S YOUR PLAN?

The second step in mastering the Money Monster is to have a financial plan.

Most people assume their monetary problems result from not earning enough. The truth is, most people earn a fortune in their lifetimes. A person who earns no more than $15,000 a year, and works for forty-five years, will earn $675,000. Someone who earns $25,000 a year during the span will earn $1,125,000. The problem for most people is not *how much* they earn, but *how they manage* what they earn.

In the remainder of this chapter, I'd like to suggest a simple financial plan that almost guarantees greater financial freedom. First, pay God. Second, pay yourself. Third, pay the bills.

A CHEERFUL GIVER? HOW TO PAY GOD

Proverbs 3:9 says, "Honor the Lord with your wealth, with the firstfruits of all your crops." That means we are to give Him the first part of our income. The Bible repeatedly suggests a minimum giving standard of ten percent: the tithe (Matt. 23:23; Luke 11:42; Mal. 3:10). Giving the tithe allows us to express our thanksgiving for the privilege of earning wages, and also graphically demonstrates our understanding that we are not the owners of our resources; we are merely stewards of the money God has allowed us to earn.

Unfortunately, many Christians get nervous every time they hear about tithing. They hate to do it—it seems like a bad debt they'll owe for the rest of their lives—yet they feel guilty if they don't. It's a classic double bind. They wonder what possessed Paul to pen the words: "God loves a cheerful giver" (2 Cor. 9:7). How could there be such a thing?

A SEED WE SOW

The answer is found in the Bible's perspective on giving. We read, " 'Bring the whole tithe into the storehouse, that there may be food in my house. Test me in this,' says the Lord Almighty, 'and see if I will not throw open the floodgates of heaven and pour out so much blessing that you will not have room enough for it. I will prevent pests from devouring your crops, and the vines in your fields will not cast their fruit'" (Mal. 3:10–11). According to Scripture, the call to tithe is accompanied by the promise that God will intervene supernaturally in the financial affairs (crops and vines) of those who consistently do. They will enjoy financial miracles that would not happen if they neglected to give to God. Therefore, giving money to God should be viewed not as a debt we owe, but as a seed we sow.

In one of the key biblical passages regarding our need to give to God, Paul relates principles of giving to principles of farming. He says, "Remember this: Whoever sows sparingly will also reap sparingly, and whoever sows generously will also reap generously" (2 Cor. 9:6).

What is Paul telling us about tithing through the agricultural habits of an unidentified farmer? He is telling us about the principles of investment, increase, and interval.

Every farmer is aware of the principle of investment: If he wants to harvest a crop, he needs to buy seed and plant it. No seed, no harvest. We need to view tithing as an investment—in the work of God *and* in our own personal financial freedom, since God blesses our giving spiritually and materially.

The farmer also understands the principle of increase: He will reap far more than he sows. A farmer who sows two bushels of wheat can expect to reap sixty-seven bushels. Three bushels of oats will yield seventy-nine bushels.

In Malachi 3:10 God promises "so much blessing that you will not have room enough for it." Jesus said, "Give, and it will be given to you. A good measure, pressed down, shaken together and running over, will be poured into your lap" (Luke 6:38).

God always promises an abundant reward to those who sow the seeds of giving. Does that mean everyone who tithes gets rich? Some people think so. They preach a "prosperity theology" which in its exaggerated form piggybacks the hedonistic American mindset and seeks to "obligate" God to prosper them financially. It's a questionable theology for two reasons.

First, the spirit of biblical teaching on giving is that we give as a multifaceted expression of worship and obedience. Scripture never promotes a "give to get rich" mentality.

Second, it limits God's provision to monetary increase. In reality,

God has many creative ways to honor the seeds we sow and intervene in our financial affairs. A young man told me of the frustration of driving an old, dilapidated car that was inadequate for the daily two-hour hospital trips necessitated by his infant daughter's chronic illness. "We couldn't afford a new car," he said, "and we didn't tell anyone we needed one. We just continued giving the tithe we'd always given, and trusted God to meet our need." Within weeks, a group of friends from church presented him with the keys to a dependable, late-model van. Through a miraculous set of circumstances, they had discovered his need and were able to raise the money to meet it.

Finally, the farmer knows about the principle of interval: He will reap after a time. He doesn't plant seed one day and harvest it the next. He patiently waits for it to mature in its own time.

Increase comes only after a reasonable interval. Too many people try to test God by saying, "Okay, I'll tithe this week. But if I don't see the increase by next week, that's it. Never again!" That approach proves two things. It proves that a person is trapped in a "give to get" mentality; he has no interest in giving as an expression of worship and obedience. It also proves he has a lot to learn about trust. Trust means we patiently wait without doubting the outcome. We obey even when we don't see immediate rewards. The principle of interval gives us the chance to prove our trust.

GOD'S ECONOMY

I believe most people would like to tithe. Deep inside they know they should. What stops them? The numbers. They trip over the math. It doesn't make sense to believe that the first step to financial freedom is to give money away. If you told that to your accountant he'd think you were crazy!

But in God's economy, it works. He says, "You trust Me with your eternal destiny. You trust Me for daily guidance and wisdom. Now trust Me with your money. I won't let you down. Sow seeds of faith and I'll meet your needs abundantly."

There are three positive results of tithing. First, churches can finance their ministries without having to resort to manipulative arm-twisting, cheap gimmicks, or secular fund-raising schemes. Second, those who tithe enjoy the benefits of divine intervention in their financial affairs. And third, the Money Monster suffers a direct hit! Giving money away is like spitting in his face. Nothing makes him shriek with agony more than the smile on our faces as we write out our checks for God's work. In writing them, we break the grip of his leash and enjoy the taste of freedom.

Several years ago I went to India to speak at an evangelistic crusade. The peasants were so poor they had to spend all their rupees on food, and I commented to a church leader that they must be frustrated by their inability to give. He said, "Oh no, they *do* give. Twice a day they boil rice for the family meal. Each time they scoop out what they need, then put one scoop in a bag. By the end of the week they have fourteen scoops of rice, which they put in the offering to be distributed to the needy."

With nothing to draw from but their own lack, these peasants choked the hoarding spirit of greed by giving what they could. If we want to defeat it we must do the same.

Common Questions Regarding Giving

1. Should I tithe on my gross or net earnings?

I believe that's open to choice, but remember: "If you sow bountifully, you'll reap bountifully; if you sow sparingly, you'll reap sparingly."

2. Where should I direct the ten percent?

Scripture teaches a concept called "storehouse tithing" (Mal. 3) which implies that we should give our tithe to the local fellowship God has called us to join. Giving beyond the ten percent is "freewill" giving and can be directed anywhere.

3. Should I tithe if I am deeply in debt and unable to pay creditors on time?

Our elders usually counsel people whose finances are in disarray to give a lower percentage until they reduce their debt enough that they're not compromising their witness to creditors.

4. Should I tithe if my spouse is adamantly opposed to it?

Giving should be a cheerful, worshipful experience. It should never become a wedge in a marriage relationship. Communicate your heart on the matter and try to work out a compromise so you can give some portion of your income without alienating your spouse.

SAVE, SAVE, SAVE—HOW TO PAY YOURSELF

Eighty-five out of one hundred Americans end up with less than $250 in cash savings when they reach sixty-five. During their working years they earned hundreds of thousands of dollars, but at retirement they have little to show for it. Why? Because all those years they paid everybody but themselves. Luke 10:7 says that "the worker deserves his wages," yet most people neglect their own pay.

The first step to financial freedom is to pay God. The second step is to pay yourself—without apology or embarrassment. How much? That varies according to earnings and financial standings, but most financial experts recommend ten percent. The miracle of compound interest assures a sizable personal savings.

Let's say you earned $15,000 a year for twenty-five years, and invested ten percent ($30 a week) in a mutual fund at nine percent. After twenty-five years, you would have $138,500. If you earned $25,000 a year, you'd have $230,809!

Years ago, Lynne and I established a personal savings account that we call our "financial freedom fund." Each week after we pay God, we pay ourselves. It's no "get-rich-quick" scheme or shortcut to financial security. But as the interest compounds, we build a reserve of funds to be used for emergencies, education, retirement, extra giving, or whatever use God directs.

Most people would rather buy lottery tickets than put away ten percent each week. Let's face it. It takes discipline to keep from spending money. It takes willpower to say no to tempting purchases. It takes a commitment to the principle of delayed gratification: enduring hardship now for the payoff later.

When Lynne and I first began to get on our feet financially, it was unrealistic to pay ourselves ten percent. Even five percent was a stretch. Because we had lived so long with no excess, it was tempting to spend the five percent on purchases we'd been wanting. But we made the hard choice to begin saving and held each other accountable when our resolve faltered.

Too many young couples yield to the temptation to spend their limited excess. And when they incur unexpected expenses, they have to borrow. That often begins their downward spiral into long-term indebtedness.

Proverbs 6:6–8 says, "Go to the ant, you sluggard [lazy man]; consider its ways and be wise! It has no commander, no overseer or ruler, yet it stores its provisions in summer and gathers its food at harvest." In other words, mimic the ant: Set aside a freedom stash in summer, so you'll be prepared for the winter. Another proverb says, "In the house of the wise are stores of choice food and oil, but a foolish man devours all he has" (Prov. 21:20). That's a creative way to say that the wise man saves, while the foolish man spends everything he has.

Money management forces us into the graduate school of character. It's hard to say no to immediate gratification. But if we cut class, if we drop out, if we're shortsighted, we'll play right into the Money Monster's trap and end up in financial frustration.

LIVE ON EIGHTY—THE WAY TO PAY THE BILLS

Giving God ten percent and saving ten percent leaves eighty percent to live on—eighty percent to pay the bills. It's at precisely this point that most people cave in. Usually it's not that they *can't* live on eighty percent; it's simply that they *won't*. They refuse to limit their living expenses. They allow glittering temptations and social pressures to push them into a standard of living that eats up all their money.

Rather then altering their lifestyle—living in a smaller house, driving an older car, buying fewer clothes, joining a food co-op—they eliminate tithing and saving. In so doing, they close the door to God's supernatural involvement in their finances and eliminate the freedom fund that would help cover future expenses.

It's bad enough that they're spending *everything* they earn. What's worse is that it's only a matter of time before they'll be spending *more* than they earn. The first emergency or unexpected expense will put them over the ledge into indebtedness.

Few people would consider driving without a gas gauge, because they know the dangers and inconveniences associated with running out of gas. Yet most people operate their personal finances without a spending gauge. They casually spend from day to day, and when they run out of money by the middle of the month, they say, "Oops! We're out. Now what do we do?"

The only way to avoid that is to use a budget. Though it's one of the most unpopular concepts in contemporary America, it's the only way to live within fixed boundaries. Every January Lynne and I agree on a realistic, workable budget. First we deduct our giving and saving. Then we deduct our set monthly expenses (utilities, mortgage, insurance, taxes, food). Finally, we determine how much we can spend on negotiable expenses (clothing, gifts, vacations, household improvements, entertainment). Then we record these set amounts and agree together not to spend beyond them.

We don't enjoy sticking with a budget any more than anyone else.

But we do enjoy the financial freedom that accompanies it. We enjoy the security of knowing that we're not going to run out of money before the end of the month or be caught off guard by unexpected expenses.

HOLY SPIRIT, TAKE CONTROL

There's not one economic lifestyle that's right for every believer. Teachers who make sweeping generalizations about how all Christians should spend their money are adding to Scripture. The Bible paints the ideal financial picture in broad strokes, offering principles that leave room for individual application. In essence, Scripture says this: "Follow the major guidelines regarding giving, saving, and spending. Beyond that, let the Holy Spirit be your guide. Let Him help you make the delicate decisions about what you buy and how you live. Only He has the ability to factor in your unique personality, profession, gifts, and stewardship abilities."

Lynne and I pray over every major financial move we make. We pray about budgeting, vacation plans, housing, vehicles, giving, and even sharing our possessions. We've learned that the Holy Spirit is amazingly capable of keeping us on the path of blessing and financial freedom. That doesn't mean He always leads us to take action that makes sense from a human standpoint. But in retrospect we can always—*always*—see His wisdom.

One of the results of financial freedom is that we have the privilege of using our excess funds to minister to others. We are free to respond to the Holy Spirit's prompting to meet a need, finance a project, or give a gift. There's nothing more frustrating than having your heart pound with the passion to offer your resources for God's use, but be in such financial bondage that you can't. For the authentic believer, financial freedom is the key, not to self-indulgence, but to self-giving.

Another result of financial freedom is that we place ourselves in a position to receive the true riches. Luke 16:11 says, "So if you have not been trustworthy in handling worldly wealth, who will trust you with true riches?"

What are these "true riches"? People. Jesus is saying that if we can't handle money, which is earthly and temporal, how can we be trusted to impact people who are God's image-bearers and have eternal and infinite value to Him?

166 HONEST TO GOD?

That inspires me! I want to pass the money management test so I can be entrusted with the privilege of influencing people for all eternity. I want to be free to offer my time, energy, *and resources* to others.

NOTES

1. Myron Magnet, "The Money Society," *Fortune* (July 6, 1987), 26.
2. Lewis Lepham, "How To Think About Money," *Forbes Magazine* 132: no. 9 (Fall 1983), 32.

13

Staying Fit:
A Glaring Blind Spot

Early in drivers' training, a good instructor alerts aspiring drivers to the dangers of blind spots. These are areas outside and on either side of a car that can't be seen in the rearview or the side mirrors. Many accidents occur because drivers fail to allow for these blind spots.

In broader usage, blind spots are any issues or concerns that are easily overlooked. In my opinion the Christian community has a glaring blind spot when it comes to physical authenticity.

Christians are outraged by certain sins against the body: sexual immorality, abortion, euthanasia, and the physical violence raging in our cities. But many Christians seem to be amazingly blind to a far more common sin against the body. With a flagrance that would be amusing if it weren't so tragic, they slowly destroy their bodies by filling them with junk foods and letting their muscles—heart included—deteriorate through disuse.

If caring for our bodies were nothing more than an act of vanity, I wouldn't waste a chapter on it. If I were convinced that God is concerned only with our souls, I would join the majority of Christians who neglect this subject. But Scripture clearly reveals God's concern about our physical well-being.

Genesis 2:7 describes that moment when the transcendent God gathered a bit of dust and miraculously and lovingly fashioned man. He breathed His very own breath into his nostrils and "Man became a living being." Then He smoothed the rough edges off man and created woman.

The human body is no fluke of evolution's process. It is God's design and handiwork. It is His masterpiece. It is the ultimate synthesis between function and beauty. Our most advanced technology pales in comparison to the capabilities of the human body.

Why did God give us these incredible bodies? So we can use them to honor Him.

First Corinthians 6:19–20 says, "Do you not know that your body is a temple of the Holy Spirit, who is in you, whom you have received from God? You are not your own; you were bought at a price. Therefore honor God with your body."

We don't own our bodies. If we're Christians, our bodies have been bought with a price. For what purpose? To house the Holy Spirit. To be a channel through which He can work.

So caring for our bodies is a responsibility we owe to God. In fact, Paul calls it an act of worship. "Therefore, I urge you, brothers, in view of God's mercy, to offer your bodies as living sacrifices, holy and pleasing to God—this is your spiritual act of worship" (Rom. 12:1).

If we are to offer our bodies as living sacrifices, shouldn't we offer them in the purest condition possible? Shouldn't we aim to offer unblemished lambs? Of course this means we should avoid immoral use of our bodies. But it also means we should do all we can to keep them healthy and useful for as long as possible.

We can do that by paying attention to the food we put in them and the way we exercise them.

NO CHEAP FUEL

Imagine that someone walked into your office, handed you the keys to a fifty thousand dollar European car, and said, "Happy New Year! This car is yours. Enjoy. One thing, though. It's an engineering marvel with a very sophisticated engine. It won't run on regular unleaded fuel. If you don't fill it with super unleaded, you'll eventually ruin the motor. So will you agree to use only the best fuel?"

Wouldn't you say, "Well, sure, that's the least I can do to show my appreciation for this wonderful gift. I'll never use anything but super unleaded!" It would be unthinkable to ruin the motor of a fifty thousand dollar car by using inferior grades of fuel. Unthinkable!

But many of us have done the unthinkable to God's engineering marvel. We've filled the incredible bodies He created, bought, and dwells in with inferior fuel—junk foods. And we've slowly ruined them inside.

Statistics bear that out. The U.S. loses nearly one million people a year to food-related diseases of the heart and blood vessels. There's also a dramatic increase in diabetes and obesity. A recent study reveals that only one in four Americans can be considered normal in regard to weight.

My own extended family provides a perfect case study. On my father's side, three uncles had heart attacks before age fifty-five. My father died of a heart attack at fifty-three. On my mother's side, two uncles died of heart attacks before the age of fifty.

When I was still in my twenties, I began having health problems. With my family history of heart disease I knew I had to take them seriously. So I radically changed my eating patterns, and the results have been tremendous—increased energy, decreased illness, weight loss, and most importantly, the knowledge that I am glorifying God by what I put into my body.

I'm not a doctor or nutritionist, but I'd like to provide a few basic guidelines for a more healthful diet. My study indicates that the greatest problem with the typical American diet is that it's too high in three elements: sugar, fat, and salt.

Sugar High

For years the health-conscious among us have sounded the sugar alarm, relating a high-sugar diet to ailments as diverse as tooth decay, obesity, and mood swings, and as damaging as heart disease and diabetes.

Aren't you glad you don't have a high-sugar diet? Or do you? The biggest problem in reducing sugar intake is that so often we're unaware of how much sugar we're actually eating.

Let's look at the diet of a not-so-uncommon junior high student. Let's say she starts her day with a "nutritious" breakfast of presweetened cereal. Mom is pleased she's eating cereal instead of a doughnut, but doesn't realize that one bowl contains 8½ teaspoons of sugar. That's a problem, especially when you add the 7 teaspoons in her white toast and jam, and the 6 in the sweetened cider she washes everything down with. It's only 7:30 A.M., and she's had 21½ teaspoons of sugar!

There's a midmorning break at school. Because Mom taught her well, she passes up the soda. But the chocolate milk she has instead adds another 6½ teaspoons.

At lunchtime she enjoys a bowl of cream of chicken soup that has 4 teaspoons of sugar. A gelatin dessert adds another 4½, and a glass of presweetened lemonade contributes a whopping 8½.

On the way home, our growing young lady passes a convenience food store. Since lunch was light, she stops in for a snack. No big deal. Just a package of frosted chocolate cupcakes and a soda—and 23½ more teaspoons of sugar!

That evening Mom's too busy to cook, so she fixes a frozen beef dinner, complete with fries and catsup. That's another 5 teaspoons, and a small dish of ice cream adds 8 more. (At least she didn't serve cherry pie à la mode. One piece would have added an unbelievable 20 teaspoons of sugar.)

Total for the day: 81½ teaspoons of sugar—on a diet sadly representative of how many young people eat.

And you know what that diet is doing to the young girl? It's killing her. Not today. Not tomorrow. But eventually a person who establishes eating patterns like that is going to pay a price—in unnecessary disease and premature death. It's an inevitable cause and effect.

The worst thing about a high-sugar diet is that it is almost always coupled with a low-fiber diet. Recent medical studies reveal a clear link between low-fiber diets and heart disease, cancer of the colon, obesity, diabetes, and various gastrointestinal disorders.[1]

So what's left after we throw away our low-fiber sweet treats? Lots of delicious high-fiber foods—fruits and vegetables, whole-grain breads and cereals, nuts, figs, dates. Fruits and vegetables not only provide natural sweetness, they also appear to reduce cholesterol levels—as do legumes (beans), oat bran, and barley.[2]

"But wait," you say. "That's what those flakes in California eat."

That's right. And I visit there a lot and see sixty-year-old men roller skating along the Pacific Coast, winking at girls on the beach. Meanwhile, forty-five-year-old Midwesterners are making their first appointment at the Mayo Clinic. Think about it.

I Like It Drippin' In Grease

My dad loved greasy fried foods—sausage, ribs, steaks, anything deep-fried. He used to say, "I like it when it tastes like it's cooked in thirty-weight motor oil. It just slides down!" He honestly didn't know his high-fat diet was killing him.

Our bodies weren't designed to digest heavy fats, so the fats settle in our arteries and clog them up, causing high blood pressure and related diseases. Recent studies also relate a high-fat diet to certain types of cancer. Can we afford to be careless about this?

Few of us enjoy a fatty diet as blatantly as my dad did. Yet many people are unaware of how much fat they actually eat.

When I talked about this at my church, I wanted people to *see* the truth about their diet. So while I described an average man's daily menu, I scooped teaspoons of fat onto a plate.

I started with breakfast—a three-egg, ham and cheese omelette— and heaped 7 teaspoons of fat on the plate. I added 6 more for two slices of buttered toast, and 1 more for a glass of milk. I didn't even suggest bacon or ham. They're ninety percent fat and ought to be outlawed!

I piled on 5 more teaspoons for a midmorning doughnut, and wondered how many men would stop at just one. Imagine what a glob of fat a long morning break could add!

Lunch was chicken à la king—7 teaspoons of fat—and more bread and rolls, which added 3. I assumed the average working man would pass up an afternoon snack, but thought he would probably enjoy the all-American dinner: roast beef with mashed potatoes and gravy. For three ounces of meat I loaded on 8 teaspoons, and for potatoes and gravy, another 5. Roll and butter, salad dressing, and cake with frosting *each* meant 3 more. A glass of milk added 1.

By then the 8-inch mound of fat was sliding off the plate.

The day's grand total was 50. Fifty teaspoons of fat that the human body cannot digest. How can we expect our bodies to function properly when they're clogged up with greasy, sticky fats?

Dairy products (whole milk, butter, and cheese), eggs, red meats, salad dressing, and fried foods should be the exceptions in our diets, not the rule. Fish, poultry, grains, brown rice, and legumes can give us complete proteins without the addition of harmful fats.

I Like Mine Salty

High-salt diets can contribute to high blood pressure, fluid retention, digestive complications, and a host of other problems. The recommended salt intake per day for the average adult is approximately 1 teaspoon. It's obvious, then, that anytime we eat at fast-food restaurants or eat packaged, prepared foods at home we are exceeding the recommended allowance.

A typical breakfast sandwich with sausage, egg, and cheese contains 1½ teaspoons of salt. A lunch of a burger, fries, and soft drink yields at least 2½ teaspoons. A quick dinner of pizza, prepared Mexican food, or frozen and canned foods would probably add another 2 teaspoons. That adds up to 6 teaspoons a day, and we haven't even considered typical snack foods—pretzels, potato chips, tortilla chips, crackers. Snacking through a football game could add another 2 or 3 teaspoons.

Medical experts tell us that anything over 1½ teaspoons a day is trouble. Yet many of us routinely take in more than eight times that amount.

To minimize salt intake, reduce your intake of prepared, frozen, and canned foods. Replace salty snacks with fresh fruits and vegetables, or homemade treats made without salt. Grocery stores are also carrying more and more "unsalted" products.

God made our bodies to function properly on pure, natural foods. How can we glorify Him with our bodies if we destroy them with a high-sugar, high-fat, high-salt diet?

Bookstores are amply supplied with excellent, easy to follow cookbooks that contain nutrition information and recipes. For those who are ready to get on the path to physical authenticity, *The New American Diet* cookbook by Sonia L. Connor, M.S., R.D., and William E. Connor, M.D., published by Simon & Schuster, is a good place to start. It outlines a gradual, four-phased transition from junk food to nutritious eating.

FIT FOR LIFE[3]

Dr. Kenneth Cooper, called "the father of aerobics," has probably done more to promote the idea of physical fitness than anyone else in the twentieth century. Dr. Cooper defines physical fitness as having a strong heart, strong lungs, and strong blood vessels. He then recommends six components that will contribute to being fit:

1. Proper weight and diet
2. Refraining from cigarette smoking
3. Avoiding all habit-forming drugs, including alcohol
4. Learning how to manage stress
5. Periodic wellness examinations, or physicals
6. Proper exercise

Proper exercise is important for a number of reasons. First, it strengthens the heart muscles and decreases the risk of heart disease. When properly exercised, the heart muscle becomes larger and stronger and able to pump more blood in a single beat. That means it doesn't have to beat as much and won't wear out so fast.

In November 1987, the *Journal of the American Medical Association* stated that a long-term study of twelve thousand men showed that those who exercised moderately (golf, walking, bicycling) on a regular basis had a thirty percent lower risk of cardiac death than those with a sedentary lifestyle. That's just moderate exercise.

The second benefit of proper exercise is that our lungs work more efficiently. Exercise strengthens the muscles that cause our lungs to expand and contract. The working space in our lungs increases, so with every breath we take in more oxygen and expel more carbon dioxide.

Proper exercise also helps prevent weight gain. With a nutritious diet and regular exercise, it's almost impossible to be overweight.

A fourth benefit is strong and healthy bones. For years people avoided exercise, fearing it would damage their bone structure and joints. Yet proper exercise actually increases the size and strength of bones and retards the brittleness and loss of bone mass that occurs in aging.

Another benefit is lower blood pressure. Though there are medications to control high blood pressure, they often have negative side effects. We ought to prevent high blood pressure naturally, through exercise, so we don't get to the point where medication is necessary.

The ultimate result of these benefits is a longer, healthier life. And these physical benefits are just the beginning. There are emotional and mental benefits as well.

A NATURAL HIGH

Every year Americans pump millions of dollars into drugs to control the effects of stress. For many people, a proper exercise program could accomplish the same thing, with little expense and no negative side effects.

You've probably heard of the "runner's high." But did you know it's more than just a psychological phenomenon? Research has proven that vigorous exercise releases a powerful hormone, endorphin, into the bloodstream. Released by the pituitary gland, endorphin is the body's natural painkiller. The "endorphin effect," which can be felt for up to two hours after exercising, produces increased energy, an improved attitude, a mood balance, and a general sense of well-being. In short, the exerciser just feels good.

I don't believe this is an accident. God knew stress was going to be a part of living in a sinful world, so He provided a natural means for us to relieve it.

Another emotional benefit of exercising results from increased oxygen intake. A study done in England showed that an oxygen increase of only fifteen percent has an antidepressant effect. It can actually relieve mild cases of depression.

In addition to emotional and mental benefits, there's the obvious spiritual benefit of knowing God is pleased with how you're caring for what He's given you. It's no small thing to be able to say, "God, I present my whole self, including my physical body, as a service of worship to You." That's my greatest inspiration for disciplined exercise.

WHERE TO START

If you are committed to physical authenticity, begin by getting a complete physical, including a stress test. This is especially important for nonexercisers or people over forty-five. The benefits of exercising become liabilities if you have medical problems you're not aware of. Please don't begin exercising without a complete physical first.

Next, educate yourself. Begin by reading Dr. Kenneth H. Cooper's book, *Aerobics Program for Total Well-Being.* Follow that with *Fit or Fat?* by Covert Bailey. The more you learn, the more you'll be motivated.

After you've been examined and educated, follow these basic guidelines:

1. Choose an exercise you enjoy enough to pursue consistently. That doesn't mean you have to love it, but you have to enjoy it enough not to dread doing it.

Dr. Cooper lists thirty aerobic exercises that can effectively shape up your hearts, lungs, and blood vessels. The top five are cross-country skiing, swimming, jogging, bicycling, and walking. I've seen many articles lately on the value of walking. It's a great way to start, because you can do it anywhere, anytime, at any age—and you don't have to learn how.

2. Schedule a time for exercise. Make it a regular part of your routine, like taking a shower or brushing your teeth. Too many people say, "When I have time, I'll exercise." But it never happens. We have to make time, write it on our calendars, and consider it a priority.

3. Watch the intensity. *Watch the intensity.* Throughout this chapter I've used the term "proper exercise" for a reason. If you overdo it, especially in the beginning, you can exhaust and discourage yourself, or even do damage to your body. If you underdo it, you won't get the benefits.

Set a goal of exercising four to five times a week, nonstop, for twenty to thirty minutes. That's certainly not too much time to invest in your health.

Exercise vigorously enough to bring your heart rate to three-fourths of its maximum. Determine that rate by subtracting your age from two hundred twenty, then take seventy-five percent of that number. That's the heart rate you want to maintain during exercise.

Many people say, "My job keeps me running" or "My kids keep me on the move." But the responsibilities of work and child care seldom boost our heart rate to seventy-five percent of their maximum for twenty minutes straight. Unless that happens, you won't receive the benefits outlined here.

Proper warm-up and cool-down are also important. Muscles forced into action too fast or not stretched out properly after exercising are much more prone to injury. The few minutes it takes to do basic stretching can prevent unnecessary complications.

4. Implement some form of accountability. Fifty percent of new exercisers quit within six months; it takes too much discipline! But it's like anything else. If you know someone is at the health club waiting

for you, or you have to give a report of your exercise schedule to a friend, you're more likely to stick with it.

Choose an exercise, schedule the time, watch the intensity, and have someone hold you accountable. It takes work and discipline, but the benefits are worth it.

Isn't it time we get serious about what we eat and how we exercise? Our goal isn't vain or temporal. Our goal is to be available for eternal purposes for the longest amount of time, with the greatest amount of energy, and the highest degree of emotional, mental, and spiritual well-being. We owe it to God to be faithful stewards of the bodies He's given us.

How about it?

NOTES

1. "Dietary Fiber and Health," Journal of American Medical Association 262, no. 4 (July 28, 1989), 542–546.
2. "Dietary Fiber and Health," 543.
3. The information on exercise was taken from a message called "Fit for Life" presented at Willow Creek Community Church by Associate Pastor Don Cousins.

14

Maintaining Authenticity

The green flag drops at the Indianapolis Speedway, and the world's most celebrated auto race begins. Gleaming, low-slung, turbocharged weapons hurtle out of the fourth turn and scream through the starting gate at two hundred miles an hour.

But give the race a little time. Driver-caused accidents, tire problems, gearbox failures, and a host of other calamities will eventually cut the field in half.

On the pace lap every car looks invincible. But it's not enough to start well. The trophies go only to those who cross the finish line.

Recent years have witnessed many people who started well but failed to end the race. In what's been called the "scandal-scarred spring" of 1987, *Time*'s cover article stated:

> Once again it is morning in America. But this morning Wall Street financiers are nervously scanning the papers to see if their names have been linked to insider trading scandals. Presidential candidates are peeking through drawn curtains to make sure that reporters are not staking out their private lives. A congressional witness deeply involved in the Reagan administration's secret foreign policy is huddling with his lawyers before facing inquisitors. A Washington lobbyist who once breakfasted regularly in the White House is

brooding over his investigation by an independent counsel. In Quantico, Virginia, the Marines are preparing to court-martial one of their own. And in Palm Springs, California, a husband-and-wife televangelist team, once the adored cynosures of 500,000 faithful, are beginning another day in seclusion.[1]

The article was called "What's Wrong?", and that's a question worth asking. What *is* wrong? Not only with our leaders, but with ourselves as well? Why do we so often start well and finish poorly? Why do we establish patterns designed to nurture authenticity, then fall back into inauthentic living?

Can we break this pattern? Can we maintain authenticity over the long haul?

I believe we can. In this chapter I want to discuss three safeguards for finishing well: discipline, accountability, and proper pacing.

A GOOD IDEA, BUT ...

Most people would agree that discipline is the key to maintaining the positive lifestyle patterns suggested in this book: prayer journaling, consistent date nights for married couples, effective service and evangelism, a balanced budget, a healthy diet, an exercise program. And most people sincerely want to be more disciplined.

But the distance between intention and reality is too often littered with frustration and failure. Good intentions remain just that. The prayers go unsaid; the date night is canceled; the honest communication is avoided; the lost do not see or hear our message; and the budget, diet, and exercise programs eventually fall by the wayside.

Discipline sounds good. But how do we make it work in real life?

Pain Now, Pleasure Later

Two words capture the essence of self-discipline: delayed gratification.

Scott Peck says, "Delayed gratification is a process of scheduling the pain and pleasure of life in such a way as to enhance the pleasure by meeting and experiencing the pain first and getting it over with. It is the only decent way to live."[2]

I couldn't agree more.

Did you ever watch a child eat a piece of cake? He eats the cake first, and then attacks the frosting. A well-adjusted kid knows the only decent way to eat cake is to save the best for last.

Later that same child learns that if he wants to enjoy after-dinner activities, he'd better finish his homework and chores right after school. Nothing ruins fun like the weight of unfinished responsibilities.

In a few years that same young man enters the job market. He starts at the bottom with long hours, short vacations, and minimal pay. But he endures the entry level pain, knowing that if he works hard he'll eventually get the payoff.

The applications to authentic living are obvious. Recently a man said to me, "I've learned that if I spend fifteen or twenty minutes early in the morning reading the Bible, praying, journaling, or listening to a tape, my whole day seems to go better. Giving up twenty minutes of sleep transforms the next sixteen hours!"

Married couples who understand delayed gratification face conflicts as they arise. They enter the tunnel of chaos, looking forward to the reward of a genuine, loving relationship.

Facing pain now to ensure pleasure later is also what gives us strength to say no to minor purchases this year so we can buy a car next year. Or to pass up dessert so we can get back into last year's wardrobe. Or to exercise in our thirties so we can enjoy better health in our sixties.

Discipline means enduring the discomfort or inconvenience now so we can enjoy the future reward.

It's Already Been Decided

Putting that principle into practice is no easy matter. It requires a commitment to *advanced decision making*.

Let me explain. I firmly believe that I will enjoy optimal energy and health only if I endure the pain of running and weight lifting. So I exercise, looking forward to the benefits it promises. That's delayed gratification. Advanced decision making enters the picture when I decide that every weekday after work I'll go to the health club. I make that decision ahead of time and write it on my calendar.

Why is that so important? Because although I've been doing this for over five years, my body still tries to revolt. Every day as I prepare to leave the office my body sends negative signals to my brain. "You really don't want to work out today. You're too tired, too sore, too busy. Just work another hour and go home. It won't hurt you to skip a day. Don't be such a fanatic."

If I had to decide whether or not to work out in the middle of that internal pressure, I'd probably never go. But I don't have to. The decision's already been made. It's on my calendar. In ink.

This practice keeps me on track in other areas too. I don't wait until 6:00 A.M. to decide whether to journal and pray. If I did, I'd push the snooze button every morning. What keeps me consistent is my prior decision to meet with the Lord every morning.

I don't wait until Thursday morning to decide about my weekly breakfast appointment with Lynne. I make that decision in January when I write her name on nearly every Thursday morning in my new calendar. If I didn't do that, it would always get crowded out of our schedules.

Lynne and I don't decide how much to spend on home decorating when a sale flyer comes in the mail. We make that decision when we plan our yearly budget. Then, if the money's available, fine. If it isn't, we don't even discuss it.

What about you? Do you decide on Sunday morning whether or not to go to church? Do you decide in the heat of an argument whether or not to aim for genuine reconciliation? Do you decide at the moment of temptation whether or not you're committed to ethical business practices or sexual purity? That won't work!

If you know you need to journal and pray more consistently, decide right now to get up the instant the alarm goes off. If you need to attend church more faithfully, decide ahead of time to go no matter how late you're out on Saturday night.

Are you heading into a confrontation? Decide now to see the conflict through to a resolve. Do you have business decisions to make? Decide now to pursue purity no matter what the price.

One of my greatest challenges is message preparation. I need to present a new message every Wednesday night and every Sunday morning. Some days I'm highly motivated to work on messages. Other days I'd rather do anything else. How do I get them done? I decide ahead of time that every Monday, Tuesday, Wednesday, Friday, and Saturday morning, from 7:00 to 11:00, I'll work on messages. Whether I feel like it or not, that's what I do. It's already been decided.

My payoff for doing that is twofold. First, I can move on to easier projects later in the day, when my concentration isn't as high. Second, I don't have to worry about standing before a congregation without a God-anointed message to give. And that's ample incentive to be disciplined.

NO LONE RANGERS

Delayed gratification and advanced decision making are important keys to authentic living. But even they are not enough. Though I treasure my independence and pride myself on being disciplined, I've had to admit my need for accountability. I've had to learn to surround myself with godly men and women who are committed enough to me to keep an eye on the way I live and challenge me when they see something amiss.

While most people acknowledge the need for discipline, many people, especially men, deny the importance of accountability. They want to be Lone Rangers. They think they can maintain authenticity on their own. They don't need help.

For years I believed that as deeply as the next guy. I thought prayer and Bible study were the only requirements for spiritual growth. But I've learned that spiritual growth is really a three-legged stool—prayer, Bible study, *and* fellowship. Our wise God designed spiritual growth to be a cooperative venture that requires the involvement of other believers.

That means significant relationships aren't luxuries for believers. They're absolute necessities.

I'm not talking about conventional friendships based on ending aloneness or having fun—friendship centered around golf or business or shopping expeditions. I'm talking about relationships centered on producing Christian character. This is the kind of relationship Paul described when he counseled believers to watch out for one another, warn one another, challenge one another, admonish one another, rebuke one another (Rom. 12:9–16).

Relationships like that sound a bit scary. We don't like the notion of others scrutinizing our lives and offering free counsel. Yet that's exactly what we need.

HELP ME

When I was chaplain for the Chicago Bears, I taught a weekly Bible study at Halas Hall in Lake Forest, where the Bears practiced. One day I arrived early and joined several players and defensive coaches who were reviewing film of the previous day's game.

Mike Singletary was running the projector. I was shocked at how often players would say: "Mike, hold it right there. What'd I do wrong on that play?"

Here were proud, highly-paid, world-class athletes saying, in effect, "Forget my fragile feelings. Forget my ego. Tell me the truth. What did I do wrong? Help me do it better."

I've played on baseball teams where hitters begged other players to tell them what was wrong with their stance or their swing. They knew they needed objective observers to analyze what they were doing.

It's common in business for a new salesman to say to a more experienced one, "If I'm ruining the presentation—tell me. I want to do it right." Or a young architect will say to an older one, "Look at this design. Can you see any problems?"

Spiritual Independence

Athletes and businessmen willingly seek help to improve their performance on the field or in the workplace. Yet many Christians refuse to seek help to improve their performance in life.

"I have a big problem with John. He accused me of behaving in a less-than-Christian fashion."

"Well, were you?"

"Yes. But I don't want *him* telling me that."

"Why not?"

"He should mind his own business. Besides, the Bible says, 'judge not.'"

Too many Christians mistakenly assume that "judge not" precludes the need for accountability. They say, "Don't make any comment about my level of commitment, my values, my vocabulary, my ethics, or the way I treat my wife, kids, or employees."

Though "judge not" does mean we shouldn't carelessly condemn others, the Bible clearly teaches the need for rebuke and admonition.

One of the greatest gifts we can have is a keeper. A keeper is someone who holds us accountable for our pursuit of authenticity. Someone who says, "I know you want to be a spiritual champion, so when I observe something in your life that's standing in the way, I'm going to bring it to your attention."

Of course we don't want casual observers playing that role. But we ought to invite one or two trusted friends to be our keepers. People who know us well and have our best interests at heart can provide a priceless service.

Recently I invited the elders of our church to point out anything in my life they felt uncomfortable with. I promised not to get defensive or reactionary. It ended up being a long and difficult conversation, but I'll never forget the important words I heard that night. Hard? Yes. But invaluable for my growth in authenticity.

You're On Your Own

Earlier in my Christian life I had many friends, but no keepers. At that time, I was routinely away from Lynne and the kids every night for weeks at a time. I was also experiencing severe symptoms of exhaustion and physical deterioration. And I had no time to pursue an authentic relationship with God. Yet no one said anything.

What's worse, some of my staff members were living the same way, and I never said anything to them.

If I tried to live that way today, I'd have keepers on me like a shirt. They wouldn't let me get away with it. And I wouldn't let my friends and coworkers get away with it either.

What brought about the change? A godly man had the courage to challenge me about my independent lifestyle.

"You're not going to make it, Bill. You're moving too fast and making too many wrong choices. You need help. You need brothers who can keep watch over your life and question you when you head down wrong paths."

He counseled me to select two or three men and form a small group. I decided to try it.

I chose three men with whom I had a strong natural affinity. I had learned through various social or ministry encounters that I enjoyed spending time with these guys. We started meeting every other week. At first it was hard to get past the weather, work, the stock market, and sports, but gradually we went deeper. We talked about what it was like growing up in our families, how we became Christians, what our vocational goals were, and what spiritual gifts we had.

Later we moved on to questions like these:

"What would your wife say is your greatest contribution to her life?"

"In what area of your life is it hardest to obey the Lord?"

"What are you most apt to lie about?"

"What Christian character trait is your trademark?"

"What trait do you most lack?"

Penetrating questions like that took us below the level of

superficiality to the level of accountability. They freed us to say the difficult but helpful things we all needed to hear.

Here are some things these brothers have said to me.

"Bill, you're not spending enough time with Lynne. What's happened to your date nights?"

"What you said in your Sunday message made you look better than we know you to be." (You can imagine how I loved hearing that one.)

"You need to move farther away from the church. Your family doesn't have enough privacy."

Some people would say those men have no business being that involved in my personal life. The fact is, those men have played a major role in keeping me in the race. I'm convinced I would have spun out of control without their loving intervention.

I recently spoke with a pastor who's a physical and emotional wreck. He's overscheduled, exhausted, and twenty-five pounds overweight. His marriage is in shambles and his kids are on the verge of rebellion.

I said, "What are you doing to yourself? You've got to quit living this way. The kingdom needs you."

He said, "No one holds me accountable. No one says anything. I'm beginning to wonder if anybody cares."

Is it that people don't care? Or is it simply that they still believe Christianity is a solo sport?

It's not. Proverbs 27:17 says, "As iron sharpens iron, so one man sharpens another." Proverbs 24:6 says that in an abundance of counselors there is much wisdom. We're not supposed to go it alone! We need each other! We need to invite godly people to be our keepers, and we need to be keepers for others.

Turn About

The other side of accountability is encouragement and support. Ecclesiastes 4:10 says, "If one falls down, his friend can help him up. But pity the man who falls and has no one to help him up!" My keepers call me to task when they need to, but they're also the ones who pick me up when I fall. And I do fall. I make mistakes, blow good intentions, and face difficulties and grief. When that happens, more often than not, God offers His counsel and comfort through the words of my keepers.

One of these brothers calls me every morning, and I know whatever I need, he'll offer to the best of his ability.

"I know you're worried about the building program. I want you to know I'm praying for you."

"What? You and Lynne are having a rough time? Just keep working at it. Don't give up."

"It's the anniversary of your dad's death. I know that's hard. I'll be thinking of you."

When I was a teenager, I was a lifeguard at a Christian camp. To make sure all the little campers survived the afternoon swim, we insisted on the "buddy system." Every camper needed somebody looking out for them.

If you and I want to become truly authentic Christians, we need to adopt the buddy system, with godly men and women watching over our lives.

TAKE IT EASY

The third key to maintaining authenticity is establishing the proper pace. If you want to control the race car you have to slow down around the turns. You can't keep the pedal to the floor and expect to finish the race.

For me that's been the hardest lesson to learn. Like many of you, I'm a high-energy, get-the-job-done type of person. I don't want to smell the flowers along the way. I just want to get where I'm going as quickly as possible.

For years I justified the pace of my life by reciting a long list of all the good and godly things I was doing. But even godly "busyness" can be destructive. When I began to see the toll my chronic overscheduling was taking on my health and family, I realized I had to slow down. I had to stop viewing life as a one-hundred-yard dash and look at it as a marathon. I had to start running more slowly, so I'd be able to run longer.

Along the way I found three good reasons to maintain a slower pace: survival, reflection, and enjoyment.

Survival

Is it too dramatic to say our very survival depends on slowing down? What do you think Jesus would say?

The first few chapters of Mark give an exciting, fast-moving account of the early days of Jesus' ministry. He had just selected His disciples and was busy training them. He was traveling, teaching, and healing people from dawn until dark. The masses were crowding around Him.

It's evident He and the disciples were beginning to feel exhausted. Then they heard the awful news that King Herod had just executed John the Baptist. In an instant, their exhaustion was overshadowed by a crushing grief.

In Mark 6:31–32 we read, "Then . . . he said to them, 'Come with me by yourselves to a quiet place and get some rest.' So they went away by themselves in a boat to a solitary place."

Jesus recognized the limitations of human capacities. "Enough is enough," He said. "You need to get away. You need to relax. If you don't, you're going to snap!"

He knew the multitude would protest. He knew people were still hungry, sick, and needy. But He also knew the disciples had reached their limit. They *had* to withdraw.

Many Christians have snapped because they exceeded their emotional or physical limits. They didn't know when "enough was enough." They tried to keep up with everybody else, forgetting God gave each of us different capacities.

Do you know your limits? Are you experiencing any of these warning signs?

— You wake up feeling overwhelmed, unable to face the day.
— You're touchy and on edge. You make mountains out of molehills.
— You're apathetic toward things that used to excite you.
— You're calloused toward others' needs or requests. You don't want to hear about people's problems.
— You develop a critical, faultfinding spirit. Nobody does anything right.
— You feel an abnormal need to withdraw from people.
— Your inner dreams and aspirations die. You have to work hard just to make it through the day.
— You have an intense desire to escape. You want to "run away from it all."
— You have a sinister desire to do something "cheap and superficial."

These are flashing red warnings: "Slow down! Relax! Get away!"

For some people that means a European vacation. For others, a quiet evening at home with popcorn and a good book. We have to experiment to discover what types of relaxation best fit our needs, schedules, and budgets.

Why is this so important? Because when we're exhausted and living on the ragged edge, we're more vulnerable to temptation and less tuned in to God's leading.

A fallen Christian leader confessed that the primary cause of his slip into immorality was that he never slowed down long enough to be refreshed and rejuvenated. The resulting emotional exhaustion made him a sitting duck just waiting for Satan's attack.

Reflection

An unknown author wrote the following lines:

I wasted an hour one morning beside a mountain stream.
I seized a cloud from the sky above and fashioned myself a dream.
In the hush of early twilight, far from the haunts of men,
I wasted a summer evening and fashioned my dream again,

Wasted? Perhaps.
  Folks say so who have never walked with God . . .
When lanes are purple with lilacs or yellow with goldenrod.

But I have found strength for my labors
in that one short evening hour.
  I have found joy and contentment,
I have found peace and power.
  My dreaming has left me a treasure,
A hope that is strong and true.
  From wasted hours I have built my life and found my faith
    anew.

I'm convinced that busyness is the archenemy of spiritual maturity. Why? Because it keeps us from reflecting. It destroys our ability to think critically about the important issues in our lives—God, relationships, purpose, goals, service.

Too many of us unwittingly fall prey to the tyranny of an unexamined life. We could use some wasted hours by a mountain stream. We'd do well to reflect on the direction of our lives.

Recently I had lunch with the president of a company with eleven thousand employees. In his eighties, he was still busy traveling all over the world, and sitting on boards and committees. In the course of our conversation, I challenged him to consider matters of eternity.

"I suppose I should give that some thought," he said.

For eighty years he'd been running, joining, serving, leading, earning, dealing, buying, and spending—but he never once responded to the Spirit's whisper to consider eternal realities.

Are you doing the same thing? Are you so taken with the treadmill that you fail to reflect on life?

It's possible you're:

— in the wrong job, or have an unhealthy perspective on your work.
— missing a leading from the Holy Spirit regarding a new ministry or calling.
— dating the wrong person or allowing your marriage to deteriorate through neglect.
— pursuing the wrong objectives in life.

These issues are worthy of serious reflection.

Several years ago I decided to take a summer study break. I realized that the "message treadmill" was wearing me out. I was managing to crank out messages, but I had lost perspective on my life. I was no longer sure of my priorities or goals. So I asked my elders to grant me a "mini-sabbatical" for a few weeks.

Lynne and I and the kids rented a tiny cottage on Lake Michigan. I spent the morning hours evaluating the previous year and looking forward to the next. I thought, prayed, planned, and reestablished priorities. By the end of the break, I had a renewed vision of the man God wanted me to be, and the ministry He wanted me to pursue.

Since then my study break has become a yearly event. Each summer I return home with fresh insights that positively impact my life, family, and ministry. I shudder to think of all I'd have missed if I'd kept my foot to the floorboard and stayed too busy to reflect.

Periodic getaways for reflection and evaluation are absolutely necessary in this fast-paced world. What about you? Why not schedule some getaway days right now? It could be the best investment you've ever made.

Enjoyment

Jesus said, "I have come that they may have life, and have it to the full" (John 10:10).

Paul tells us that God "richly provides us with everything for our enjoyment" (1 Tim. 6:17).

One more value of slowing down is that it lets us rediscover the joy in life—the fun, the laughter, the pleasure. We do this best as we embrace the gift of play.

> Play is more than just non-work. It is one of the pieces in the puzzle of our existence, a place for our excesses and exuberances. It is where life lives in a very special way! . . . In play you can abandon yourself. You can immerse yourself without restraint, you can pierce life's complexities and confusions. You can become whole again without even trying![3]

God created certain activities for the express purpose of letting His children experience a taste of the delights of heaven while still here on earth.

I love talking with people who enjoy the "excesses and exuberances" of play. Their eyes sparkle and they can't hide their smile.

"You should have been there. The sun was shining. The landscape was lush and green. And on the first tee I hit a perfect drive!"

"What an experience. That little bay pony ran like there was no tomorrow. Her mane was dancing and her tail was flying. She enjoyed the day as much as I did."

"It was wonderful. I curled up in an easy chair, and for two hours I was lost in another world. Page after page pulled me into an adventure I'll never forget!"

For some people it's golf, horseback riding, or reading fiction. For others it's bicycling, fishing, snowmobiling, car racing, camping, or snorkling. For you it may be knitting, ant farming, or worm wrestling!

Who cares? What's important is that every now and then we plunge headlong into one of our great leisure loves. For me that's sailing. One of God's most lavish gifts to me is that He led a man in my church to give me free use of his sailboat in the Virgin Islands. Because of my schedule, I only use it twice a year, but those trips refresh me like nothing else does.

For most of the year I'm consumed with responsibilities and demands. Even when I'm not technically at work I'm often thinking about messages, meetings, or building programs. The only time I manage to leave all that behind is when I'm sailing. There's something about the wind and the water that wash every trace of concern from my mind and truly fill me with the exhilaration of play. I come home totally refreshed and revitalized.

Do you have a leisure love? Have you suppressed it? Do you feel guilty about enjoying it?

Don't! God wants us to enjoy pleasure and refreshment. He wants us to taste a bit of the goodness of heaven in the here and now. The stereotyped picture of the stodgy old Christian with sunken eyes and sagging shoulders is not the picture God wants us to paint with our lives. He wants us to be authentic people who exhibit authentic joy.

NOTES

1. Richard Stengel, reported by David Beckwith, "What's Wrong?" *Time* 129, no. 2 (May 25, 1987), 14.
2. Scott Peck, *The Road Less Traveled* (New York: Simon and Schuster, 1978), 18.
3. Tim Hansel, *When I Relax I Feel Guilty* (Elgin, Ill.: David C. Cook Publishing Co., 1979), 63.

Conclusion

What is an appropriate ending for a book on authenticity?

It seems to me it should show the vital, consistent faith of people who live above the weak, surface, confused Christianity too often characteristic of our day—authentic Christians who mark our lives with their strength and integrity.

I just folded up a letter from a new Christian who explained that his devotion to Jesus Christ cost him his high-paying job because he could no longer condone his boss's unethical practices. He said his new job pays less and requires a two-hour commute. But he claims that a clean conscience is worth the inconvenience and loss of status. That is authentic Christianity.

A man I work with questioned me today about a comment I made that offended him. He dared to express his honest feelings to me, his supervisor, and risk the consequences of telling the truth. By the time he left my office, we had cleared the air, settled a misunderstanding, and preserved our relationship. That is authentic Christianity.

This morning I learned of a woman who finally worked up the courage to tell her small group about her emotional trauma resulting from child abuse. She openly admitted that her past was straining her marriage to the breaking point. The group members gave no sermons. They accepted what was shared and offered to listen as long and as often as their friend wanted to talk. Then they embraced her and prayed. That is authentic Christianity.

A friend dropped by my office today on his way to the airport. He and his wife were sneaking away for their annual "honeymoon." After thirty years of marriage, the flame of their romance blazes higher than ever. That is authentic Christianity.

A commodities trader called today to say he would accept my challenge to teach a stewardship seminar at our church. He is a millionaire who lives modestly and gives lavishly to Christian endeavors worldwide. That is authentic Christianity.

Over lunch a real estate broker told me about a man in his office who had just become a Christian. Over the years my friend had prayed for that man, expressed sincere interest in his personal life, and earned the right to talk to him about his faith. That is authentic Christianity.

Last night during an elders' prayer meeting we prayed with the sick in our church. As I had many times before, I prayed with the parents of a severely autistic child. Tearfully they shared both their heartache and their trust in God's prevailing power and goodness. That is authentic Christianity.

This evening when I got home I enjoyed a relaxing dinner with Lynne and the kids. I listened to the comfortable tabletalk and thanked God that years ago a few friends loved me enough to point out what my overscheduling was doing to my family. I came so close to missing out on so much. But now here, in my home, I can experience one of my biggest doses of authentic Christianity.

What qualifies me to have written this book on authenticity?

You have read just a few of the reasons in the preceding paragraphs. Years ago God surrounded me with authentic Christians whose integrity and vitality revealed my inauthentic lifestyle for what it was. Their examples of Christlikeness provided an unrelenting challenge to my immature and inconsistent attitudes and actions. They did more than just talk Christianity. They lived Christianity in their relationships, their ministries, their finances, their leisure, and their work.

God has given us the instructions for authenticity, the guides who can point toward it, and the supernatural power needed to bring it about in our lives. It's up to us to take the first step on a journey from which we'll never want to return.